Grace Notes

MEDITATIONS FOR WOMEN IN THE CHURCH

RUTH N. KOCH

Abby —
You are God's grace note!
Love, Mom
7.10.97

CPH.
SAINT LOUIS

To David, who made me a pastor's wife

Copyright © 1997 Concordia Publishing House
3558 S. Jefferson Avenue, St. Louis, MO 63118-3968
Manufactured in the United States of America

Library of Congress Cataloging-in-Publication Data

Koch, Ruth N.
    Grace notes : meditations for women in the church / Ruth N. Koch
      p.   cm.
    ISBN 0-570-04974-1
    1. Spouses of clergy. 2. Women in church work. 3. Spouses of clergy—Prayer books and devotionals—English. 4. Women in church work—Prayer books and devotionals—English. I. Title.
    BV4395.K63 1997
    242'.692—dc21   97-6815

1 2 3 4 5 6 7 8 9 10   06 05 04 03 02 01 00 99 98 97

Contents

Grace Notes

Let us run with perseverance the race marked
out for us. Let us fix our eyes on Jesus.
Hebrews 12:1–2

Tabletop Moments

Sergei's brother emigrated from Siberia to America.
He wasn't allowed to write home about America so the
two worked out a code.

Sergei would send a photograph.

If life was not so good, he would have his right hand
in his pocket. If life was good, he would raise his right
hand.

When the photo arrived, *Sergei was standing on a table,
both hands raised!*

In a picture of how you feel about being in public ministry, would your hand be in your pocket? Raised? Or
would you be atop a table, both hands in the air?

Actually, tabletop moments are rare. They surprise
you.

Mostly, public ministry is daily obedience. Eyes on
Jesus. Quiet joy. Showing up. Hand up. Hand in pocket.
Prayerful diligence. Commitment for the long haul.

Trying to climb up on that table can make you crazy.

And then, surprise! One day you're atop a table, both
hands raised—*in praise to God!*

*Dear God, thanks for the gift of salvation and for sup-
plying quiet joys and everything I need for the long haul. And
thanks for those occasional great moments atop a table. All
praise to You!*

Try This: When you have a "tabletop moment,"
record it for your own encouragement.

The grace of our Lord was poured out on me abundantly. 1 Timothy 1:14

Abundant Grace

The woman stared at us.

My little Easy Rider in the grocery cart said, "Mom, she goes to *church.*"

I thought I recognized her. She *knew* she recognized me. *She was surprised.*

Then the familiar words I hate to hear. "Well, I guess pastors' families have to eat too!"

I manage a smile. There's a battle within.

It feels lonely when members are surprised that you need lettuce and toilet paper. What's the surprise?

Beats me.

They're attempting conversation with a person they perceive as a minor celebrity. They don't know it sounds like we're an oddity, some weird species.

They *do* want to bridge the gap they think separates us.

Jesus died to build a bridge across the chasm of sin that separated us from God. I don't deserve such lavish, abundant grace.

Members are trying to make a social bridge, and I want to honor that with the same grace God has given me.

Dear Lord, thank You for building a bridge to save me. When people want to build a social bridge to me, bring gracious words to my lips and love to my heart, even though I may feel lonely and set apart.

Try This: Believe those first awkward attempts at conversation mean good will.

We struggle and work hard, because we have placed our hope in the living God, who is the Savior of all. 1 Timothy 4:10 TEV

My Bed ... And Welcome to It

She stole my baby bed.

She left town, and my bed went with her.

This wasn't just *any* baby bed. It was a lovely red bed—with beautiful, intricately worked spindles.

After our second daughter, I loaned it to Cherise. And she stole it.

I loved that bed.

Surely an indigent, single mom needed it more than I needed to keep it in the attic for grandkids still decades away.

Public ministry serves people who have desperate needs. They also may have character flaws. And sometimes it costs what you don't want to pay. Like a beautiful red baby bed.

Then the cost of public ministry gets personal.

Has the love of people who stocked her pantry and furnished her apartment and, yes, loaned her a beautiful red baby bed spoken *her Savior's* love? Does she know God's generous love because some church people generously loved her?

I won't know till heaven. But that's my prayer.

Living God, Savior of all, keep me focused on what public ministry is all about: introducing people to their Savior. Help me when I struggle with the cost of doing that.

Try This: If someone has taken something you didn't want to give, ask God to bless it so it becomes an instrument of His saving grace.

11

I will be glad and rejoice in You; I will sing praise to Your name, O Most High. Psalm 9:2

Sunday Morning Martyrs

"Do we have to go to church *every* Sunday?" the kids whine. Their friends don't. My friends at work don't.

An unasked question gnaws at me.

If I weren't the wife of a church professional, would I go to church *every* Sunday and insist that my kids do too?

It feels like my husband's profession closes off my permission to choose.

Internal war. One side delights to sing praise to God and wouldn't miss worship for the world. The other side wonders whether I would choose *this* congregation. *Every* Sunday? For the kids? For myself?

How does spousal obligation-to-support, the need to "train up" our children, and the expectation of others influence my church attendance? My attitude?

Truth is, no matter what my husband does for a living, I need the Holy Spirit's guidance to decide about my spiritual life, my worship, my commitment to the God who has eternally committed Himself to me.

Just like everyone else.

O Most High, thank You for Your eternal commitment to me in Jesus. Show me how to make spiritual commitments because of Your love for me, separate from any other obligations.

Try This: Next Sunday, notice when being "the _____'s wife" distracts you from worship. Ask God to help you focus.

[Speak] the truth in love. Ephesians 4:15

Go Ahead—Be Crabby

Life *is* difficult. People are difficult. Sometimes *we're* difficult.

No wonder we need a Savior!

But must church workers always be *cheerful?*

Christ bought our salvation with His life and death, and we have eternal comfort in difficult times. We have deep joy—not necessarily perpetual smiles.

Whine a little. Be crabby every now and then.

But when crabby, do not sin.

God made us *response-able,* able to choose responses. Choose crabby if you want. It's your choice. No one makes you crabby.

Here's crabby in a spirit of love: "I'm crabby because I had to stand in a long line only to be sent to another line!" "I'm crabby because I need more sleep." "I'm crabby because life isn't going the way I want and I want my way!"

Those are okay crabbies—"I statements" that don't blame or accuse, only describe.

Be real. Have a bad day. Whine a little.

Be crabby ... in a spirit of love.

Lord Jesus, thank You for holding me close, even on the most exasperating, disappointing days. Help me live as a real person embraced by a real Savior who loves and comforts me.

Try This: Change accusing "you statements" into descriptive "I statements."

Each of you should look not only to your own
interests, but also to the interests of others.
Philippians 2:4

My Needs Are Your Pleasure

Rugged individualists have a hard life.

You see, I'd much rather *give* help than ask for it. You
too?

In the face of a problem or calamity, my first response
is to dig deep and use the resources God has given me.

Rugged individualists get scolded a lot. We hear a lot
about pride, sinful attitudes, and ungodly reasons for not
being more dependent.

St. Paul affirms that you are to look out for your own
interests. That's healthy independence.

You also get to look out for others. That's healthy
*inter*dependence.

And here's the twist. One way to meet the needs of
others, to give them pleasure, is to allow them to help
when you need a hand. You know what a pleasure it is to
serve someone!

Spread the fun around and allow *inter*dependence.
Serving and being served are privileges of the Christlife,
marks of a life redeemed by a crucified, victorious Savior.

Even for rugged individualists.

*Dear Lord, I want to do it myself. I am sorry for the times
I pretend I don't need You and others. Show me how to be
responsibly independent—and open wide to the joys of being
interdependent.*

Try This: When you are reluctant to ask for help,
trust in the other person's pleasure in serving you.

14

The cheerful heart has a continual feast.
Proverbs 15:15

How Is a Cowboy Like a Saucepan?

They're both at home on the range!
Did you laugh? Or smile? Or maybe groan?

Unless you have regular contact with a grade-schooler, you may not hear much silly humor. If so, that's too bad.

Public ministry sometimes exposes you to lots of real-life ugliness. In the midst of heartbreak and pain, life doesn't look like a continual feast.

You need to deliberately *cultivate* a sense of humor. Funny movies. Great cartoons. Neat stuff your kids say. The absurdity of life in the spotlight for all to see.

Laughing is better than a coffee break.

Laughter is God's gift to church workers and their families. It helps you keep your balance so you can serve desperate people desperately in need of Good News. Good News of Christ the Savior.

Now *that* brings a smile to the lips and makes a heart merry!

By the way, why doesn't Sweden export cattle?
Because she keeps her Stockholm!

Lord of the universe, regularly remind me that You are God and I am not. Thank You for my Savior, Christ the Lord. Refresh me with an appreciation for the funny parts of life.

Try This: Find a book of cartoons or jokes and refresh your sense of humor.

From now on we regard no one from a worldly point of view. 2 Corinthians 5:16

Awed by Riches

On Christmas Eve 1928, Charles Gauss announced the gift of a new Trinity Church as a thankoffering for the miraculous healing of his daughter from polio. The result was a miniature cathedral of such architectural beauty that it remains one of Detroit's artistic gems.

The gift of ... *a new Trinity Church!*

What a generous witness to God's goodness!

From a worldly point of view, a gift like that invites you to be a bit awestruck. Awestruck by members who have that much money.

Comparisons are inevitable. Church workers notice the monetary gulf between the haves (them) and the have-nots (you).

How about a faith point of view that leaves you awestruck at *God's* riches!

From a faith point of view, both the wealthy and not-so-wealthy need a Savior and have been graciously redeemed by Christ's blood. Monetary considerations are not considerations!

Every redeemed person has reason to generously and daily offer God thankofferings—*for the riches of salvation.*

Heavenly Father, I am awestruck when I consider Your generous gift of Jesus! Help me keep a faith point of view when I feel like a have-not.

Try This: Today give God a personal thankoffering of time, talent, or treasure.

Everyone should be quick to listen, slow to
speak and slow to become angry. James 1:19

This Is Not about You

Vessie's got a bee in her bonnet.

In fact, Vessie's had a whole colony of bees in various
bonnets for years. Vessie delivers complaints, champions
underdogs, loves to tell you what's wrong. Even people
who *don't* want her help get it.

Vessie complains to leaders. That's you—or your
spouse.

You're supposed to apologize for the problem, clean
up the mess, and make it all better. And make sure it
doesn't happen again.

Vessie personalizes her complaints so it sounds like
Vessie thinks *you're* responsible for everything.

You take a deep breath when you see her coming.

What if you set aside your personal defenses and ask,
"What does Vessie's behavior tell me about Vessie?"

If this weren't about you, it could be about *Vessie.* And
you could personalize it in a way that blesses: quick to
listen, slow to speak defensively, slow to anger.

You could serve Vessie personally—as you are served
by God's sweet love in Jesus.

*Lord God, thank You for Your gracious and saving love in
Jesus, my Savior. Show me how to get my defenses out of the
way so I can love the Vessies of my life as You love me.*

Try This: Make a "Vessie List" of all the people who
stir up your defenses. Ask God to help you love and serve
them.

17

Don't grumble against each other. James 5:9

Little Grumbles

Who cares if you don't like the new chancel carpet?
Brace yourself.

Lots of people care. And they'll spread the word.

It's a basic principle of leadership: *Anything negative you say will be repeated.*

Because you're in public ministry, a juicy little negative from you is big news. Valuable conversational currency.

It would be a privilege to say little grumbles like everyone else. It isn't fair to be quoted every time you express a negative opinion, but it's the way things are.

Sharing those little grumbles provokes side-taking and invites people to have an opinion about *you.*

Do your part to stop the subtle negativism that mars the beautiful body of Christ. A body most precious, redeemed by Jesus, your Savior.

Save your little grumbles for the person in charge, your best buddy in your hometown, or your sister in another state.

Then, when you've got a big grumble, it'll be *good* to know people are listening!

Lord Jesus, I am sorry for the times I have been unmindful of my leader role and have contributed to negativism in Your church. Guard my tongue so the words I speak build up Your body.

Try This: When you've got a little grumble, stop and plan the most effective way to share it.

Then [Jesus] returned to His disciples and
found them sleeping. Mark 14:37

After All I've Done for Them!

You knock yourself out being the best wife, mother,
homemaker, church worker's partner, den mother,
employee, volunteer, neighbor, citizen, and church member you can be. Then there's the extra mile, the extra
smile, the one more thoughtful gesture.

There are so many needs, so few people to be ser-
vants. You want to belong, contribute, serve. *I'll do the best
I can,* you say.

One day you cross an invisible line. You realize you
are thinking uncharitable thoughts. That many people
neglect thank-yous. That you feel used instead of useful.

Resentment creeps in and exhaustion blankets every
day.

Imagine Jesus in the garden. After all He had done
for them! *Before* the awe-full things He would do for their
salvation ... the disciples, asleep!

Three times He found them asleep.

He was human and exasperated. He was God and
stayed the course.

Go ahead, scale back. Make a sensible, realistic,
healthy lifestyle. God likes that.

And remain a servant.

*Dear Jesus, my Savior, forgive me when my busyness dis-
tracts me and I neglect my physical and spiritual health. Help
me find a balance in my serving that pleases You.*

Try This: Give up one existing activity each time you
take on a new activity.

When the Chief Shepherd appears, you will receive the crown of glory that will never fade away. 1 Peter 5:4

Have You Been Poofed?

Here comes a loving fairy godmother, wand in hand. *Poof!* You're a principal's wife, Queen of the School!

There's genuine honor for your husband, sincere regard for the ministry you both provide. Lots of love and warm gratitude. Cooperation. Those occasional moments in the spotlight are quietly gratifying.

Some days, however, it feels like you've been just poofed, not crowned. Being queen isn't all it's cracked up to be.

Hard choices, hard work, difficult people. Disappointment. It's a struggle to stay on course, to love.

Crowns don't motivate. Magic wands can't sprinkle fairy dust on the difficult realities of ministry life.

Jesus, the Chief Shepherd, is the only one who hands out real crowns. The crown that comes *after* the faithful service.

Those *poof!* crownings only distract. And make it harder to keep your eyes on Jesus.

Enjoy the loving, well-meaning fairy godmothers. But wait for your real crown. When Jesus returns.

Dear Lord Jesus, thank You for the sincere regard many people have for me and my husband. Help me focus on the crown You will give and not be distracted by crowns that fade away.

Try This: When someone wants to crown you queen of something, receive the love and remember the crown of life is the only one that lasts.

Foxes have holes and birds of the air have nests, but the Son of Man has no place to lay His head. Luke 9:58

No Place Like Home

"Now I don't have any home to come back to!" your daughter angrily shouts, awash in the pain of the impending move.

No place like home ... no place that just stays put while all of life changes. It's not just kids who feel that way.

Church workers can feel like nomads. With frequent moves, no place feels like home. A little permanence would be a very good thing. Make that a lot of permanence.

Jesus knows how you feel. Jesus knows how your kids feel. Jesus had no place like home, no place to lay His head.

So how could He be at peace? How could He keep working, serving, and sacrificing toward the goal of our salvation? Why wasn't He empty, bitter, and scared?

Jesus focused on His only home, heaven. He sacrificed everything so you could be there with Him.

So you could be home. A place of permanence.

At last, a place that's home.

Lord Jesus, sometimes I feel like there's no place that's home ... until I remember my heavenly home. Thank You for living, dying, and rising so I could be there with You.

Try This: Remind yourself that no matter how long you live there, *every* earthly home is temporary.

Be strong and take heart, all you who hope in
the LORD. Psalm 31:24

A Life of Quiet Desperation

"Of all the people who come to our counseling
agency, church workers' wives are the most desperate."

A quiet desperation, the counselor calls it.

Cautious about discussing family problems in the congregation or fearful of denominational officials, a church
worker's wife may feel alone and desperate.

She may even feel isolated from her husband who,
absorbed in his work, may not be nearly as concerned as
she is about family or personal problems.

Is quiet desperation inevitable? Only if you insist on it.

But women are resourceful people!

Start with the one who knows and loves you best. Ask
Him to help you find a confidant. The same God who
cares for you eternally and sent your Savior, Jesus, provides for your everyday concerns.

Quiet desperation doesn't have to be. You must shake
the bushes, peer around corners, make some test runs.
Take the initiative.

Get out there and find someone to talk to!

*Dear Father, thank You for loving me and sending Jesus
to be my Savior and friend. Show me how to be active and
hopeful as I try to deal with my loneliness.*

Try This: Plan an activity and ask someone *outside*
the church to join you. Ask God to help you be a Christian witness as you make a friend—and be one.

It is better to be patient than powerful. It is better to win control over yourself than over whole cities. Proverbs 16:32 TEV

Mount Comfort's New Bus

Mount Comfort's new church bus is a special model for committees: It comes with one gas pedal, four steering wheels, and 10 sets of brakes!

What challenges church workers' patience more than a committee meeting? *Several* committee meetings in one day!

Might the secret of true church work happiness be a totalitarian state? The church worker as emperor, your people as slaves. Sounds good, doesn't it?

Well, fleetingly.

Committees are valuable *and* exasperating for the same reasons: People get a chance to have their say and to put their personal stamp on ministry.

Maybe God has similar thoughts as He looks over what *you* do and how you do it.

"I still have to watch those church workers like a hawk," He says. "They think they know what I want at Mount Comfort. I've been telling those laypeople specifically what I want for months now, but the church workers keep trying to control things!"

Humility invites patience.

God of my salvation, I confess that my impatience is sometimes grounded in my deeply held belief that I usually know better than the people You have given me. Because of Jesus, forgive me and give me a humble spirit.

Try This: When you're in a committee meeting, silently thank God for the strengths each person brings to the task.

23

Let the peace of Christ rule in your hearts,
since as members of one body you were called
to peace. Colossians 3:15

Praying with Your Eyes Open

The youth minister sits down with the youth board, ready to begin with prayer. After hesitating, he looks up and says, "With our current hard feelings, would anyone object to my praying with my eyes open?"

Not funny when trust is strained and the atmosphere charged with criticism. Not funny if you've wanted to watch your back and speculate about peoples' motives—while waiting for the other shoe to drop.

Not funny if you've been there.

Not much Christian peace ruling in your heart. Doesn't feel like one body united for ministry.

Truth is, whether it *feels* like it, we are indeed declared one body and are indeed called to peace—by God Himself.

Open your eyes to the truth that God wants you to live in peace. Focus on the unity Christ bought with His lifeblood, His life sacrificed to make you brothers and sisters.

Then close your eyes and pray.

God of peace, I want the peace of Christ to rule in my heart and in my behavior. Help me be a leader who models that peace, especially in the midst of hard feelings.

Try This: Learn about Christian conflict management.

"I will say to those called 'Not my people,' 'You are my people'; and they will say, 'You are my God.' " Hosea 2:23

The Kindness Squad

One summer Friday evening, weekend gridlock had cars backed up for a quarter mile to the church's corner. The outreach minister and his Kindness Squad swung into action.

After icing down 400 cans of soda, they offered free cold drinks to drivers sitting at the stoplight.

To the inevitable, "Why are you doing this?" their response was a friendly, "Because God loves you."

A seasoned Kindness Squad, they had reached out in more than 40 creative ways in the previous six years: free car washes (leaving notes under windshield wipers), free pictures of families in the park (a sticker on the back gave the church address and phone number), free coffee (and tract) at a grocery store, to name a few.

They are *always* asked, "Why?"

What does it take to say to those called "Not my people" that God declares, "You are my people"—so they can say, *"You are my God!"?*

Lots of loving creativity, fresh thinking—and bright ideas!

O God, You are my God! What a free and wonderful gift is Your salvation! Show me how to speak the Gospel to others as personally, practically, and lovingly as You have spoken it to me.

Try This: This week, ask God to give you fresh thinking and bright ideas.

The Lord is my helper; I will not be afraid.
Hebrews 13:6

Nerves of Steel

Catherine Pradier. Beautiful, sophisticated, dedicated. The most valuable agent the Allies had in France as the D-Day invasion drew near.

Catherine was to infiltrate Gestapo headquarters and plant doctored military intelligence. Time was short. Reports of her real identity were quickly catching up with her.

Spies fascinate. They often possess extraordinary personal qualities. Nerves of steel. Fearlessness. Single-mindedness.

What do nerves of steel look like for church workers, *God's* front-line operatives?

- The Good News mission is urgent—*you do what needs to be done.*
- Time is running out for the unsaved—*you get to the point.*
- God is our helper—*you are not afraid.*

Unbeknownst to Catherine Pradier, her mission was designed to distract the Gestapo from the Normandy landing—by making them prepare for a landing in Calais, as she had been told. She, however, played for keeps.

God's mission is straightforward. To play for keeps He gives nerves of steel.

Helper, Savior, and Lord! Thank You for my Savior, Jesus, and the mission You have given me. Show me how to be single-minded, fearless, and ... nervy.

Try This: Be aware of the temptation to ignore the urgency of bringing the Good News to those whom you serve.

When you pass through the waters, I will be
with you. Isaiah 43:2

Some Creatures Grate and Appall

The advertisement in the university newspaper urged
pre-med students to enroll in a test preparation course.
The test service offered this comfort, should the student
fail to qualify for medical school.

*The candiru is a tiny parasitic fish that swims
into one's urinary tract and extends its spines
into the urethra, causing excruciating pain. Once
there, it is impossible to dislodge.*

*We tell you this so that, if you don't get into med-
ical school, you will know that there are others
suffering more than you!*

Does anyone suffer more than professional church
workers? *What a silly question.*

Yet sometimes your preoccupation with the difficulties, disagreements, and troubles surrounding your work
makes it seem like you have a corner on suffering.

It's futile to focus on those who have it worse to make
yourself feel better.

To gain a truly useful perspective, focus on the God
who saves, comforts, and encourages you by keeping His
promises. No matter how tough the going gets.

*Dear Father, thank You for fulfilling all Your promises in
Jesus, my Savior. Teach me to look to You for genuine comfort
and encouragement.*

Try This: When you experience the waters, remember Isaiah 43:2.

Therefore confess your sins to each other and pray for each other so that you may be healed.
James 5:16

Combine Your Gifts

Opposites attract, we're told.

If you're married, you know it.

Two *very* different people get married because they think they are so much alike. Then they give up celebrating the similarities and start noticing the differences.

Then they may embark on a plot, mostly below awareness, to make the other person more like themselves.

The plot buster is prayer. Praying *together.*

"It is only when a husband and wife pray together that they find the secret of true harmony," says noted physician Paul Tournier.

Praying together challenges you to seek *God's* will and relinquish your attempts to dominate each other.

Confessing sins to God in each other's presence offers the privilege of assuring each other of God's forgiveness.

Being honest before God—together—invites intimacy and honesty.

And there's a bonus. Praying together helps you realize that two very different people can *combine their individual gifts* instead of setting them against each other.

God of healing and grace, thank You for the life You bought with the blood of Jesus. Bless the daily discipline of praying with my husband that we may experience harmony. Teach us to enjoy and appreciate our differences.

Try This: Identify one difference and consider how it blesses you.

Do what is right and good in the LORD's sight, so
that it may go well with you. Deuteronomy 6:18

Dig the Well before You're Thirsty

A lot of life is about getting ready. Clean the house for
a party. Buy birthday cards to send next week.

The least frazzled among us think ahead and shop or
research or pray to get ready for what is coming.

So it is with spiritual life. Whether you realize it, every
day you're getting ready, digging the well, planning for
the unexpected event, accident, catastrophe, or life-
changing blessing.

Especially for church professionals, the watchwords
are *daily obedience* and *spiritual discipline.*

Before you're thirsty, dig the well through regular worship, constant prayer, consistent Bible study, faithful
attendance at the Lord's Table. Be reminded daily of God's
gift, Jesus.

Bring an open mind and heart. Be greedy for God's
resources, impatient for God's riches.

God will prepare you for the dry times of life.

Then when your throat is parched and your spirit is
withering, drink the Living Water God gives and be eternally refreshed!

*Living Water, Savior, and Lord! Thank You for Your faith-
fulness and Your commitment to sustain me through the dry,
parched times of life. Increase my self-control and spiritual
discipline and make me ready for what lies ahead.*

Try This: When things are going well, recommit yourself to daily spiritual disciplines.

Make it your aim to live a quiet life, to mind your own business. 1 Thessalonians 4:11 TEV

Leap In. Limp Out.

I knew what she was doing wrong in her family. She was trying to control her husband and kids. And reaping the whirlwind. Just like Scripture says.

I should tell her.

I prayed about it. Made my plan. Practiced my words, trying to mix gentleness, compassion, and straight talk.

I could see best from the outside, I reasoned. I could be really helpful.

She didn't thank me. In fact, she rather politely threw me out. Not a bad idea, as I think back on it.

Leap in. Limp out.

She hadn't asked for advice, and she *did* suggest I mind my own business.

I know now that I hadn't earned the right to intervene. I hadn't built a genuine relationship with her. I hadn't spent enough time praying and listening to God. And I was pretty impressed with myself.

My need for Jesus is what I have in common with others. Jesus helps me stand next to, not above, others.

Dear Lord Jesus, I am sorry for the times I have stood above others in judgment and pride. Thank You for Your example that teaches me how to love generously and humbly. Show me how to mind my own business in a way that pleases You.

Try This: Need does not equal a call to intervene. Take the time to pray about someone's need until it becomes clear how to act on that need.

But God has shown us how much He loves us—it was while we were still sinners that Christ died for us! Romans 5:8 TEV

Astounding, Abounding Grace!

Warning: Occupational Hazard. Church workers and their families may become immune to joyful outbursts brought on by God's grace.

St. Paul thought the Gospel he told the Romans warranted an exclamation mark. An outcry of strong emotion!

It's a privilege to study God's Word so you can teach it, preach it, and reach out with it. There's certainly a lot to learn about theology and doctrine. There's a lot to *think* about.

But there's more to the Good News than good thinking.

God wants to be the God of your whole person—body, intellect, emotion, spirit.

Meeting our Savior, Jesus, leads to exclamatory living. Energy. Vigor. Dancing for joy. Sometimes tears. Enthusiasm. Astonishment. Hymns of thanksgiving on the way to the grocery store.

> *Break forth my soul for joy and say: "What wealth is come to me this day! My Savior dwells within my heart: How blest am I! How good Thou art!"*

Have you become immune to the *wonder* of salvation?

Thank You, Lord Jesus, for the salvation Your life and death and resurrection affords me. Thank You for the gift of faith. Refresh me again and again with the wonder of it all!

Try This: Spend time each day worshiping God because of His free gift of salvation in Jesus.

I will praise the Lord, who counsels me. Psalm
16:7

I Feel Like a Failure Today

Yesterday I asked for honest feedback. And got it.

I heard glowing praise and affirmation of my work.
And five or six kindly worded suggestions for improvement.

Whacked me out, those kindly worded suggestions for
improvement. Sent me down to the bottom of the pit.

I feel like a failure.

At the same time, I am exasperated to be traveling this
route of hypersensitivity again. Embarrassed at my lack of
balance. Dismayed that I am so painfully sensitive to criticism when I can spout with the best of them all the benefits of constructive criticism, lovingly offered.

How many times do I have to review the lesson, Lord?

Let's look at the truth just one more time: No one's
perfect. I'm not perfect. In gracious love, You sent my
Savior, Jesus, for just that reason. Because Jesus was perfect *for* me, that perfection counts as mine.

Ah! Peace with God. Peace within.

If I'll let God counsel me.

*Lord, thank You for being so patient with me. I'm sorry
that I keep wanting to rely on my perfection when Jesus paid
dearly on the cross for my peace. Show me how to receive
with gratitude the gift of criticism—and learn from it.*

Try This: This week at worship, hear God's forgiveness with new thanksgiving.

I will pour out My Spirit on your offspring, and
My blessing on your descendants. Isaiah 44:3

Life in a Gold Fishbowl

His classmates were at it again. This time the cruel
kid humor was about the movies he doesn't get to see.
They like to point out how his family is different.

"I hate this place!"

"I hate those kids!"

"I hate you and Dad for all your rules!"

"I hate living in a goldfish bowl!"

It doesn't do any good to try to explain that our values
and choices are *Christian,* no matter where his dad works.
For him, the issue is his dad's shadow and being an example and having lots of people know what you do with your
life. The goldfish bowl of public ministry.

Sometimes you're lonely in that goldfish bowl too.

But God did promise His Spirit to your offspring and
His blessing on your descendants.

And Jesus is the guarantee that God keeps His
promises.

God transforms your goldfish bowl into a *golden* fishbowl—where you live under God's promise and blessing.

*God of promise, in the most difficult times, I trust Your
faithfulness. Thank You for Jesus who is no stranger to the
fishbowl of public ministry. Give me wisdom to know how to
answer my children who don't see the blessing and promise.*

Try This: When you see something golden, remember God's promises.

See, I have engraved you on the palms of My hands. Isaiah 49:16

I Want You to Meet My Pastor's Wife

Through the crowd I see her pushing toward me, elderly parents in tow. I know what will happen next.

"Mom, Dad, I want you to meet my pastor's wife."

That's it. She's done.

It would be natural to add my name, "my pastor's wife, Ruth."

Maybe she doesn't know my name or can't remember it.

More likely, she doesn't think a name is necessary. It's enough to be "my pastor's wife" or "our principal's wife" or "the choir director's wife."

Just think. A whole population of women out there without first names!

Puzzled at first, I waited for my name, the cue to respond.

Then I felt annoyed to be regarded as an accessory.

Now I understand that a churlish pastor's wife is a poor witness to the God of love and graciousness who has my name engraved on His hands. *That's* where my name really counts.

Now I smile, extend a hand. *Hi, I'm Ruth. Welcome.*

Dear God, I'm sorry that I sometimes get in the way of Your plan to love people through me. Thank You for writing my name in the Book of Life. Show me how to give up my annoyances and be Your gracious lover.

Try This: Challenge yourself to learn one new name each week. Then use that person's name when you greet him or her.

34

For God did not give us a spirit of timidity, but a spirit of power, of love and of self-discipline.
2 Timothy 1:7

The Chronically Shy Need Not Apply?

Marlene's terrified. She's going to the ice-cream social, but she's not afraid of calories. Marlene's painfully shy.

People assume that church workers are at ease in every situation. Marlene was aghast to find that people depended on *her* to make introductions, construct social bridges, and maintain conversations. She's frequently nudged into the spotlight and expected to behave like a seasoned performer.

What if you're a shy church worker? Or a church worker's shy wife?

If indeed the chronically shy need not apply for church work, most of us should be doing something else. Thank God social ease is not a criteria for serving God's people!

Christ's love motivates us. But an urgency for the Gospel propels us—even into uncomfortable social situations. So the shy can be effective in public ministry, God's Spirit gives courage and power and self-discipline.

When properly motivated, even the shy can shed their cocoons!

Lord, sometimes I feel so shy that I'd like to stay home. Help me trust Your promise of courage, power, self-discipline. Remind me of my world's urgent need for salvation. Make me willing to do what it takes to share the Gospel.

Try This: Read a book about how to mingle, make small talk, or overcome shyness.

Each one should use whatever gift he has received to serve others, faithfully administering God's grace in its various forms. 1 Peter 4:10

I'm Not Dorothy

Dorothy always had the door open, the coffee pot on, and a willing ear. Dorothy was *available.*

People just loved Dorothy, and Dorothy loved them back. She knew how to talk their language, a language that made people feel comfortable and connected.

Did I mention that Dorothy played the piano?

Dorothy also was my predecessor in a small rural congregation. I was a newlywed, terrified of making mistakes, painfully inexperienced. I lacked the maturity and experience that would make me an attractive person to sit down with over a cup of coffee.

And I don't play the piano.

Dorothy was a formidable act to follow.

I spent those first years self-centeredly focused on what I couldn't do and who I wasn't. I repent.

Thanks to God for Dorothy and her gifts. And thanks to God for you and your gifts. And thanks to God for my gifts.

And, thanks to God, we're each equipped to do ministry in a most unique, delightful way!

Father, I'm sorry for the time, energy, and ministry I waste when I compare myself to others. Thank You for Jesus who makes me Yours. Help me treasure the ministry gifts You have given me.

Try This: Think of someone whose gifts for ministry you envy. Thank God for that person and write a short note of appreciation.

When Jesus had finished these parables, He moved on from there. Matthew 13:53

Busier than Jesus

Jesus was always swamped with work. Lacking a home base, He improvised meals, securing lodging as He went.

And His helpers needed a lot of supervision. His Twelve often were confused and bickered among themselves.

He knew His mission: He was to live a perfect life, *be* the love of God, heal the sick, redeem the lost, comfort the afflicted, and afflict the comfortable.

His commitment to make God's enemies into friends was always on His mind. It would take a perfect life, agonizing death, and triumphant resurrection.

Jesus was busy.

You're busy. Maybe you're even busier than Jesus.

But Jesus didn't struggle with time.

No wristwatch, you say?

No, Jesus didn't have to readjust priorities. Your salvation was His number 1 priority, and He moved obediently, single-mindedly, straightforwardly to accomplish it.

Everything He did advanced that purpose.

Maybe you're busier than Jesus because you haven't yet identified the number 1 priority.

Lord Jesus, thank You for Your single-minded commitment to my salvation and to the salvation of the world. Help me clearly identify and claim the ministry You've set before me. Keep me purposeful and dedicated.

Try This: Spend time in prayer identifying and claiming the ministry God has set before you.

"Are you still so dull?" Jesus asked them.
Matthew 15:16

Aarruuugh!

Jesus was exasperated!

The Master Teacher had just taught with great clarity a powerful, uncomplicated lesson. He even used the Bible-time equivalent of, "Read my lips."

We know that even the Pharisees got the message—because the Pharisees were offended.

Later, Peter, speaking for the disciples, said to Jesus, "Explain the parable to us."

Aarruuugh!

What a temptation to sin! And Jesus was without sin.

Jesus was not, however, without exasperation. But He expressed it without sin. Then He patiently explained again.

I'm thankful for that glimpse of Jesus with real people. Jesus knew He would have to die to cover the sins and hard hearts and dull spirits of His hearers—and you and me.

Jesus loved them *and* was exasperated with them. At the same time. And then He got back to the business at hand, the business of teaching God's will.

It's the Jesus way to love. In ministry to real people.

Lord and Savior, I'm sorry for the many times I have sinned in my exasperation. Stir up in me the love You have for the people in my life. Show me how to be honest and loving when I am exasperated—and how to get on with ministry.

Try This: Learn to say, "I am exasperated!" rather than denying it.

Where two or three come together in My
name, there am I with them. Matthew 18:20

Lord, Are You Sure?

Just off the boat. The new principal and his family
arrive in a foreign land. Well, it isn't really a *foreign* land.
It just seems that way.

This is not the familiar urban scene. The small town
and its surrounding farms seem to invite each family
member to a different fear.

The people are all related in some way—and they
wear funny clothes.

Time is used differently here. People visit in homes.
There are no complicated carpool schedules. They play
board games.

Skepticism is evident on the other side as well. One
congregational pillar informs the Mrs. that, "We were hop-
ing for an older man. But we'll make do."

Lord, are You *sure?*

Try as they might, there is no denying the divine call
to ministry in this place. So here they are. In the midst of
God's people. Dear people for whom Christ died. With
more in common than anyone would ever dream.

And One in common—for eternity.

*My Savior, Jesus, thank You for Your saving grace that
joins me to people You love in every place and circumstance.
Your presence blesses and unites us! Help me look for all the
things we have in common.*

Try This: When you are in a new place with new
people, look for the common experiences of life and faith
that can be bridges to relationships.

39

Those who trust in the Lord are like Mount Zion, which cannot be shaken but endures forever. Psalm 125:1

You're the Only One I Can Tell

We sat at my kitchen table, our kids played nearby.

"You're the only one I can tell," she said quietly. And then her story. Grief. Betrayal. Secrets.

Quite a remarkable woman.

I marveled at her artfully hidden wounds. Courageous. Responsible. Lonely with her burden.

But not lonely anymore. She had invited me to glimpse her inner life.

What a privilege. How do I qualify?

Strangely, first because of my *husband's* job. A church worker's wife surely must share his Christian faith and values, she told me. Then she looked *me* over, to see faith and safety. Because I live in a glass house, she got a good look.

What a privilege that my gift of faith blesses her gift of faith. What a privilege to be like Mount Zion for her— someone who trusts God and won't be shaken.

A privilege realized because God chose to use me. A ministry opportunity *because* I'm married to a church worker.

Lord, You are like Mount Zion! Thank You for being my firm foundation, unshakable and enduring. Strengthen my faith so my unique position in the church serves and blesses many.

Try This: Notice the unique ministry opportunities you have because you are married to a church professional.

Forget the former things; do not dwell on the past. See, I am doing a new thing! ... I am making a way in the desert and streams in the wasteland. Isaiah 43:18–19

New Beginnings

We've moved to a new community—lock, stock, and barrel. Boxes, bikes, and flowerpots. Not a pretty sight.

I'm not even sure I want to be here. I liked it back there. We had friends, and I knew how to live there.

Although I am certain of God's call to ministry here, I know a part of me lags behind.

Moving requires total relocation—achieved over many months.

The part of me that is back there needs to be fully present here. I'm called to live in the present. In this place. At this time. In ministry with these people.

I couldn't have a new beginning *anywhere* if God hadn't given me a new beginning in Christ, my Savior.

Now that God has made me eternally secure, I can trust Him for everyday security. He wants to do a new thing here. He will supply everything I need.

Even streams of water in the desert.

Thank You, Savior, for my new beginning, Your gift bought by Your lifeblood. Thank You for providing everything I need to serve and be happy in each new place. Help me forget what hinders my willingness and ability to begin anew.

Try This: When faced with the challenge of relocation, list the things that *won't* change.

As the Scripture says, "Anyone who trusts in Him will never be put to shame." Romans 10:11

The Best-Smelling Version of Yourself

A television host described his job: "Every night you're trying to prove your self-worth. It's like meeting your girlfriend's family for the first time. You want to be the absolute best, wittiest, smartest, most charming, best-smelling version of yourself you can possibly be."

Every night a race against shame, a contest between demons of disgrace and humiliation.

This is not about putting one's best foot forward. This is about earning love.

Consider being a church worker in the public arena. Consider the yearning to be loved.

God doesn't tell you not to care what others think. But while you're caring, you're to put your *trust* in God.

God knows your foul-smelling self. Christ's death on the cross was a sweet-smelling sacrifice. And now you belong to God because of His *undeserved* love, His grace.

Even when you're less than the best-smelling version of yourself, God loves you. You'll never be put to shame—because Christ was.

Dear Savior, I confess that I spend a lot of time and energy trying to earn love and avoid shame. Thank You for freeing me from that bondage by experiencing the full force of the shame I deserve. Show me how to live that good news!

Try This: When you're being hard on yourself, expecting a *perfect* performance, remember the good news of God's undeserved love and approval.

42

Our citizenship is in heaven. Philippians 3:20

I Want My Good-Bye Back

There's a country song about a man who broke up with his girlfriend. Tormented, he visited a psychiatrist. When the doctor saw a picture of the former girlfriend, he asked for her phone number. Now the fellow wants his good-bye back!

I don't know that poor fellow's chances of reversing his breakup, but there have been times when I've wanted my good-bye back.

Forty million Americans relocate each year. Many of them belong to our congregations, attend our schools, sing in our choirs. We know and love one another.

Then they move. And we stay.

I hate seeing the taillights of people I love as they pull out of the driveway for the last time. I'm tired of the heartache.

I want my good-byes back.

God has comfort. God offers me the long view: Christians are joined for eternity by faith in Christ. Through His grace, there's never a final good-bye. I'll get my good-byes back in heaven!

Lord, thank You for walking with me through the grief of saying good-bye. Thank You for the comfort of knowing that, because of Christ, we will be together in eternity. Help me continue to invest myself fully in the people You've given me.

Try This: Today remember one person who has moved away. Write a brief note of appreciation and encouragement.

Encourage one another daily. Hebrews 3:13

Give Mary Sunshine a Rest

He's down in the dumps, says he's going to work at a gas station and give up church work. He's tired of criticism, long hours. Some days are like that.

Time for Little Mary Sunshine to spring into action? Deliver the Buck Up! speech? Make him smile again?

This time don't talk. Listen.

His feelings belong to him and not to you. While they may threaten your security (you never wanted to marry a gas station attendant?) or exasperate you with their illogic, his feelings and thoughts deserve a hearing.

Listening and encouraging demand objectivity. So get a life that isn't *centered* on how he's doing.

Of course you care. Deeply. But refusing him down time because *you* feel anxious only increases his pressure.

When you are less anxious and pressuring, he is challenged to manage his feelings effectively.

Invite him into the healing Sonshine of God's Word. Pray together. Listen.

Give Mary Sunshine a rest.

Jesus, my Comforter, I'm sorry for trying to manage other people's feelings so I'll feel better. Help me center my life on the eternal comfort You give me. Show me how to manage my anxiety so I can serve others well.

Try This: When someone you love expresses discouragement, listen carefully and at length, then offer to pray together.

I Don't Recall Asking for Advice

It's a marvel.

Our kids act up in church and people offer advice about how to raise them.

My husband good-naturedly complains about the summer heat and several women advise me that he should wear only cotton shirts and I should launder them frequently. They've apparently talked it over.

We plant favorite flowers around the parsonage and people offer advice about what we *should* have planted and what we should do now to water, weed, and cultivate.

I'd like it if they first tried to determine what I know or what my plans are or what I'm thinking. That would be a *conversation*.

Unsolicited advice rains freely on those in public ministry!

It helps to remember that unsolicited advice belongs to the giver and doesn't necessarily imply criticism. Some want to fix everything. Some offer advice to everyone. Some think I'm their daughter. Some just don't think to ask if advice is welcome.

I want to be kindhearted and kind*mouthed*.

God of infinite kindness, thank You for showering me with Your lovingkindness by sending my Savior, Jesus! Help me curb my annoyance and speak kindly when I am offended by unsolicited advice. Show me how to use what I can and, with the breath of kindness, blow the rest away.

Try This: Practice nondefensive phrases to use when you receive unsolicited advice: "That's an interesting idea." "Thanks for thinking of us." "We'll consider that."

Be very careful, then, how you live ... making the most of every opportunity, because the days are evil. Ephesians 5:15–16

Be Very Careful How You Live

Life in the glass house, the goldfish bowl, or in the public eye is a challenge. Especially if you have kids. Especially if you're human.

You're aware that *they* are aware.

Everyone has an occasional bad day or publicly misbehaves. I'll bet you can remember with great accuracy the last time you lost your temper at church.

But note that St. Paul tells *every* Christian to "be very careful how you live." If you weren't in professional church work, you'd *still* have to curb your sinful behavior, be careful of your everyday witness.

The reason is sobering: because the days are evil. Paul doesn't say you should behave yourself because everyone's watching and you'll avoid picky, petty criticism.

St. Paul invites you to passionate, intense, *deliberate* Christian living because it's at that moment that people who are awash in evil times will meet their Savior.

Lord, I'm sorry for the many times my life has not been the witness You desire. Thank You for forgiving my sins and giving me the Holy Spirit's power to live to please You. Help me seize every opportunity to live for You.

Try This: Each time you hear a news report about how evil the times are, pray for courage to live a life that makes a difference.

Parents ... raise [your children] with Christian discipline and instruction. Ephesians 6:4 TEV

The Kids' Club

A cartoon shows a volunteer in the church nursery looking up from diaper duty, saying, "I would never have expected the DCE's child to have a diaper like THIS!"

Whether your kids are pastor's kids, principal's kids, missionary's kids, teacher's kids, or other select members of the Kids' Club, kids of professional church workers can have a tough time because of unreasonable expectations.

Although those expectations are unreasonable, irrational, and maddening, people still hold them. Sometimes it sounds like conditional love.

But if you will discipline and instruct, your children can experience valuable training.

It is under Christian parents that children learn the unconditional love of God in Christ, their Savior—and learn to be most concerned about *God's* expectations.

Even if you belong to the Kids' Club.

And, as a Kids' Club bonus, our children learn to forgive people for their mistaken thinking and their unfair expectations.

And *that* is a life lesson of great value.

Dear Lord Jesus, forgive me when I am most concerned about what our congregation thinks of our kids. Thank You for claiming our children as Your own in Baptism. Show us how to be godly parents who teach our children what You desire.

Try This: At home, talk openly about how the things God desires may differ from what congregation members expect.

On that day tell your son, "I do this because of what the LORD did for me when I came out of Egypt." Exodus 13:8

Reputation Anxiety

Pastor David Seamands talks about raising his kids in the church community: "I always told our kids that we would not spiritually or emotionally blackmail them to maintain my reputation as a pastor."

Wow!

Such a promise to one's kids takes an enormous amount of courage—and faith. It requires giving up the what-will-people-say motivation and embracing the motivation of the Gospel.

Your privilege is to tell your kids that God has accomplished salvation in Christ Jesus, that He continues to sanctify us by His Spirit's power, that He will take us home when Jesus comes again in glory.

God has brought you from a far country to be at home with Him. Parents have to know it first, then pass it on. *First as joy, then as primary motivation.*

In grace-filled homes, parents in public ministry can manage their reputation anxieties without resorting to spiritual or emotional blackmail.

By the grace of God, it can be done!

God of grace, I am sorry when I try to motivate my children to good behavior by using Law and blackmail. I want to live so immersed in grace that everything I do speaks Gospel. Thank You for Jesus who forgives and enables me.

Try This: Sometime soon, in a very simple, personal way, share your faith with your child.

God is able to make all grace abound to you,
so that in all things at all times, having all that
you need, you will abound in every good
work. 2 Corinthians 9:8

All That I Need

A family used to be called shiftless if they lived from payday to payday. Now they're excellent financial managers!

In the money-tight lives of professional church workers, finances cause worry, disagreement, and resentment.

We worry about our children's education. Husbands and wives disagree about how to use limited funds. Resentments can mar a relationship with a congregation that may be able, but unwilling, to appropriately compensate a well-educated, dedicated worker.

Financial problems sometimes overwhelm us.

Still, God's promise is that you will have *all that you need*. In all things. At all times. So you will abound in every good work.

It's hard to abound in good works when you're worried and resentful. That's why you're told, *God is able to make all grace abound to you*. Jesus is the assurance that God's grace abounds in everyday life and for eternity.

You have all you need ... so you can get to work.

God of abundance, I'm sorry for the times I worry about what we do not have. Show me how to trust You for our everyday provision—as I trust You for eternal life. Thank You that Your grace reaches every part of my life!

Try This: Remember a time that God wondrously provided money for an important need. Share that story with your husband, good friend, or children.

49

Better to live in a desert than with a quarrelsome and ill-tempered wife. Proverbs 21:19

Not Me?

Vintage joke for either gender: "My wife has the worst memory." Oh, yeah? Forgets everything? "No. *Remembers* everything!"

If you live with such a person, it isn't funny. But a bit of *self*-examination is instructive.

I like it when people get along, and I often help.

But I sometimes hang on to hurts and injustices after they could have died a natural death. I'm pretty good at CPRing old wrongs. Makes me ill-tempered, chronically annoyed at people who should have done better or known better.

And even though it's good to discuss problems, sometimes I don't know when to quit. I keep trying long after the other person is exhausted. I probably seem quarrelsome.

My family hasn't voted to move to the desert yet. That's good.

I want to speak up, work on problems and deal with the past—in a way that pleases God and lives out His graciousness.

And keeps my family from eyeing the desert.

God of forgiveness, I'm sorry for the times I'm quarrelsome and ill-tempered. Thank You for forgiving me because of Christ's atoning death. Teach me how to manage conflict in a way that pleases You and serves my family well.

Try This: When you're ruminating about an old grievance, stop and ask God to help you work on a plan to address it—so you can deal with it and give it up.

For it is shameful even to mention what the disobedient do in secret. Ephesians 5:12

Keeping Secrets

What a spring day! Welcome sunshine, gentle breezes wafting sweet lilac scent, tulips everywhere.

I was working with a church in conflict, interviewing a former pastor to learn the church's patterns, milestones, and hear his version of the congregation's history.

Early in the interview, he offered: "I could tell you dirt about the leaders who are causing trouble now. They've got skeletons in their closets."

It took my breath away. *No pastor ever tells a person's secrets.*

Momentarily speechless, I stared blankly. Surely I had misunderstood. But he was talking. And I wasn't mistaken. I declined his offer and soon ended the interview.

The day's sweetness highlighted the bitter reality of sin. Kind of like the Garden of Eden gone bad.

People trust you with their secret sins. And they trust you when you tell them God forgives those sins. Your personal integrity and trustworthiness help them hear the Gospel.

It's an awesome privilege. An awesome responsibility.

Dear Lord, it is sometimes tempting to tell secrets. I claim Your promise of Your Spirit's power to resist that sin. Guard my lips. Make me a person who can be trusted with secrets and with Your good news of salvation.

Try This: When you are dying to volunteer the inside scoop, stop, count to 10, and ask God to enlarge in you His fruit of the Spirit—self-control.

They were saddened, and one by one they said to Him, "Surely not I?" Mark 14:19

They Have to Ask!

It's Jesus' last supper with His beloved disciples. He knows what's coming. His heart and thoughts are full of it: betrayal, humiliation, suffering, death, descent, rising.

As always, He is single-minded, utterly committed to the task. Intense.

It slips out, without drama or accusation. "One of you will betray Me."

The disciples are aflutter with speculation. They have to ask. "Surely not I, Lord?" Each asks because each knows he is capable of the unthinkable. They have to ask.

What happens? In the company of people who didn't know what was about to happen and who wouldn't understand even as it unfolded, Jesus loves with an everlasting love. He makes a new covenant written in body and blood, given for forgiveness of sins.

Jesus offers forgiveness for all the sins they had committed. And all the sins they knew they were capable of committing. Such bitter self-knowledge craves grace.

Lord Jesus, thank You for Your gift of forgiveness, even when I daily betray You. Grant me the gift of self-knowledge, the awareness of original sin and all its possibilities. Then fill me with the assurance and joy of Your salvation!

Try This: When you hear of a member's sin and are tempted to tsk-tsk, ask God to make you aware of your capacity for unthinkable sins.

Man's anger does not bring about the righteous life that God desires. James 1:20

Slighted

First I was hurt. Then I was mad. For years, I was chronically annoyed.

Maybe it's happened to you. At the wedding, the bride's parents say: "We sure hope you and your wife are planning to join us at the reception and dinner. We'd love to have you."

Early on, my husband would call me at home, and I'd scramble furiously to find child care and get ready. We didn't know how to refuse such a well-meaning (though obviously second-thought) invitation without hurting *their* feelings.

In my Mad Period, I focused on their awful manners. Miss Manners would take to bed with the vapors!

When I quit trying to protect their feelings, we learned to graciously decline.

Now, we still decline—but work to keep the relationship intact. Even people with social lapses need their Savior.

God graciously covers with Jesus' blood a lot more than my social errors. I want to do the same for others.

Thank You, Holy Spirit, for giving me a yearning to accomplish Your will on earth. I'm sorry for the times my desires and hurt feelings have gotten in the way. Show me how to overlook other peoples' slights so Your will can be accomplished.

Try This: When you receive a last-minute invitation, feel free to accept or decline, according to your honest personal preference.

If your brother sins against you, go and show
him his fault, just between the two of you.
Matthew 18:15

I'm Mad at Your Husband

What a convenience for people who are mad at your
husband. They have this nice lady (you) who will listen
objectively and relay the complaint to the offender. Con-
venient. Safe.

Maybe they think you've had a feeling-ectomy and
aren't defensive when someone criticizes him. Maybe
they think your silence is willingness. Maybe they just
don't think.

No matter, you need to know that you are being
offered a rare opportunity *to help someone sin.*

God's Word clearly tells us to complain directly to the
person with whom we have a grievance. You encourage
the complainer's disobedience by carrying the message
yourself.

God promises to bless your relationships by blessing
your obedience.

You don't have to listen to people complain about your
husband. In fact, you *shouldn't.*

Give people the chance to experience God's blessing
for themselves as they speak directly, share forgiveness,
and enjoy the unity Christ's blood bought us on the cross.

*Lord God, thank You for Your clear word about how to
settle grievances. I confess that I often have helped people sin
by letting them talk to me and not to each other. Help me
learn to graciously direct people to speak with each other.*

Try This: Practice raising your hand and politely saying, "Excuse me for interrupting, but you're really talking
to the wrong person. You need to tell my husband, not me."

Forgetting what is behind and straining toward
what is ahead, I press on. Philippians 3:13–14

Frozen Anger

Resentment is frozen anger.

You've been genuinely offended at church, and you don't know how (or it feels too risky) to address it directly. So you keep your anger inside and feel hopeless and helpless.

It seems safer to freeze your feelings.

But untended anger sends a chill through your heart, a hint of indifference into your relationships.

The anger becomes like permafrost—permanently frozen subsoil. Not visible on the surface, but God knows it's there. Perma-anger.

How does a frozen heart warm again? Where is warmth for chilled relationships?

Only a warmhearted Savior could melt the permafrost of our resentments.

Only a warmhearted Savior who has endured the permafrost of eternal separation from God and risen victorious could move you to intentional, God-pleasing amnesia.

Only a warmhearted Savior could move you to confess your cold-hearted resentments, warm you with forgiveness, stoke up the courage and resolve to address future wrongs directly so you can *press on.*

Lord, I've carried my frozen anger so long that it seems comfortable and justified. I repent and ask Your forgiveness. Show me how to address wrongs directly and immediately so I can press on in warm and loving ministry.

Try This: Pull out one frozen anger and ask God to help you address it and let go.

Where your treasure is, there your heart will be also. Matthew 6:21

It's All Going to Burn Up in the End, Anyway

Author and speaker Mary Whelchel tells a poignant story of standing in the chancel after vandals had set fire to the new baby grand piano and recently refurbished organ she delighted in playing. They harmed nothing else.

With broken heart and sinking spirit, she surveyed the ruined instruments. At that dark moment, she heard a small voice in the back of her mind, "You know, Mary, it's all going to burn up in the end, anyway."

Even without dramatic tragedy, you know the wonderful material possessions God has given are transitory.

You arrive naked and leave naked. No pockets in your shroud.

God blesses you with comforts and grand things. Then He sends more. Occasional luxuries. Surprises great and small. Everything you need. Then more.

And it will all burn up in the end.

It's a system of faith economics. What you can see will burn up. Jesus, the treasure you can't see, endures eternally.

Jesus, priceless treasure, You are so good to me! Thank You for so many material provisions and the comfort and pleasure they bring. Most of all, thank You for the gift of salvation guaranteed by Your death and rising.

Try This: What would happen if you spent as much time today nurturing your spiritual treasure—your faith—as you do caring for your material treasures?

Join with me in suffering for the gospel.
2 Timothy 1:8

Disturbing the Peace

I like things nice, neat, and comfy. I like it when people like me. I want people to like my husband and my kids. I especially like it when they like my dog.

I'm one of those people who learned to "make nice" when I was growing up. Smooth over the rough spots. Let's all be friends and get along.

I'm especially uncomfortable when faithful ministry requires disturbing the peace.

At times, Gospel ministry invites us to say the unpopular thing, speak a clear word of judgment, or urge movement in a direction that generates anxiety.

None of us wants our peace disturbed.

Church work is not for cowards. Strike that. Make it: *Church work is for cowards who trust God to save, direct, and protect them.*

When I trust God, the suffering and the disruption inherent in Gospel ministry makes eternal sense.

For the sake of the Gospel, I can stand to have my peace disturbed.

Father, thank You for saving me and calling me to be a partner in Gospel ministry. Show me how to minister courageously, even when it disturbs my peace or the peace of those I serve.

Try This: Next time your peace is disturbed because of the Gospel, read 2 Timothy 1:1–18 for encouragement.

Clothe yourselves with humility toward one
another. 1 Peter 5:5

Don't Go Away Mad

Doug and Carrie were quite a "catch." Active leaders,
creative, smart. Such gifts for ministry! Everybody liked
them.

And they liked *us*. They chose us. We were proud.

Now they're on their way out. And they've made it
plain that they don't like us anymore. They have a long
list of grievances. They don't want to stay to work them
out.

And they're bad-mouthing us. Just as they told us
about their previous congregation. We believed them, so
others probably will believe them about us.

But I can't easily dismiss them, even if this is repeat
behavior.

Pride blinded us to their real ministry needs. We
viewed them as people without problems or sins. That's
pretty bad theology.

*God's Word assures that we're all humbled by our sin and
need for a savior.* God in love sent Jesus to save us. No
exceptions.

Even if people *seem* bigger-than-life.

It's a painful lesson to review.

*Lord Jesus, I confess that I was blinded by pride. Now I'm
heartsick because we missed a ministry opportunity. Thank
You for forgiving me. Show me how to serve in humility,
understanding that our need for a Savior unites us.*

Try This: When people leave in anger, remember to
bless them on their way and continue to pray for them.

They built a fire and welcomed us all because it was raining and cold. Acts 28:2

A Sight for Sore Eyes

Hot. Humid. Home alone with the kids. *After* housework, the pool beckons.

I smell like I'd been playing soccer before the invention of deodorant. The mirror shows a woman on the verge.

The girls drag out every toy in the house, and I am grateful they're playing happily without me. *I need to keep working.*

Of course that was the doorbell. And nowhere to hide!

Former members of the congregation. Clean, dressed up, calm. Enjoying a few vacation days. Couldn't be in town without stopping by.

"You get one apology, only *one*," I tell myself.

"Watch your step, there, and come out to the kitchen. It's been a busy morning. You're certainly a sight for sore eyes!"

Even on hot summer days, it's a cold, inhospitable world out there. So God built a fire and welcomed us all.

Now we can focus on important things. Like people. And set aside temporary embarrassments.

They hug me at their own risk.

Lord, thank You for a home where the fire of Your love provides warmth and comfort. Give me the grace to know when to set aside my concerns so I can warmly welcome and enjoy Your people.

Try This: When you're caught unprepared, apologize only once.

Show true humility toward all men. Titus 3:2

Tell Your Husband for Me

"Oh, would you tell your husband for me ...
... I won't be at Elders Monday night."
... I'm going into the hospital on Wednesday."
... Mother's cancer is back."
... My dad had a stroke. Tell Pastor he's at St. Joe's."

I used to take messages after church, before church, in the store, and through the car window in the preschool parking lot.

I wasn't very good at it. Occasionally I got the message wrong. Or I didn't see my husband until it was too late. Sometimes I remembered to pray for the people but *forgot to tell my husband.*

Once I forgot to relay a surgery date, and the family was furious that my husband didn't show up. Make that *livid.*

It is humbling to admit my limitations. But it's necessary for effective ministry.

Now I *help* people deliver their messages. That's good because it gives my husband a great opportunity to share God's comfort with people who are scared, angry, or worried.

Lord, I'm sorry for the times I've ignored my limitations and people have been hurt or felt disregarded. Thank You for forgiving me and helping me learn lessons in humility.

Try This: Practice useful suggestions such as, "I know my husband would want to talk with you" or "I'm so sorry. I know my husband would want to hear that from you" when you think the person needs to deliver the message.

If you suffer as a Christian, do not be
ashamed, but praise God that you bear that
name. 1 Peter 4:16

Of Course You'd Say That

It was a great opportunity to speak faith where I work.

Like a child whose allowance burns a hole in his pocket, I was eager to talk about the God who saves and sustains me! *God, help me be natural and calm.*

I was amazingly brief. Others may talk about the stress of witnessing, but this was pure joy!

And the response?

"Of course you'd say that. Your husband's a minister."

The silencing put-down. In two short sentences she cut to the quick.

I think church workers and their families have an opportunity to suffer uniquely. If what we say is indeed congruent with our life's work, people may be skeptical.

It's the strangest double bind: discounted if you *do* live faith, suspected if you *don't.*

Church worker or not, Peter's advice is still *do not be ashamed.* And praise God that by His grace we bear the precious name *Christian.*

Speak up! And leave the skeptics to God.

Christ, my Savior, it is such joy to belong to You! Show me fresh ways to speak of Your love and salvation to unbelievers. Keep me urgent about sharing Your love, even in the face of withering skepticism.

Try This: Remind yourself of all the people who have sought you out *because* you were affiliated with a church.

When we were God's enemies, we were reconciled to Him through the death of His Son.
Romans 5:10

Upside Down and Backwards

We carry inside ourselves an instinctive barter system.

You scratch my back; I'll scratch yours. You have to give to get. You only get out of it what you put into it. There's no free lunch.

After the fall, life became a barter system. It makes sense. No wonder it's difficult to grasp the beautiful simplicity of the Gospel.

That God chose to love and save us *while we were His enemies* makes no sense to a people hooked into paying for, deserving, or making trade-offs for benefits received.

It seems upside down and backwards.

Then there are those golden moments when the Holy Spirit provides insight and faith, when it makes humbling, magnificent, grace-filled sense that God chose to offer His enemies reconciliation.

It was the terrible death of God's Son that changed the rules and bought enemies eternal reconciliation. Reconciliation claimed by the gift of faith.

Now God's upside down is the only way to be rightside up!

Holy Spirit, thank You for giving me the gift of faith at Baptism. And thank You for those golden moments when I know God's love and forgiveness with great clarity. Show me how to tell God's Good News in an upside-down, backwards world.

Try This: Occasionally stop to reflect that *normal* in our world is actually upside down and backwards in relation to our Christian faith.

Be kind and compassionate to one another,
forgiving each other, just as in Christ God for-
gave you. Ephesians 4:32

I'm Married to a Difficult Man

I don't complain about my husband to church members and staff. I think it invites disloyalty and might hamper his ability to minister to them someday.

I save my complaining for *him*—and our dog—and
occasional grumbling and mumbling under my breath.

Oh, yes, I'm married to a difficult man. He conducts
Big Tidy Ups without provocation, has stubborn opinions,
and frequently cancels my vote in national elections.

Actually, my husband could rightly say he's married
to a difficult woman.

Christian marriage is a mystery. In the face of individual differences, we're called to be kind, compassionate,
and forgiving. *Because God in Christ forgives each of us.*

So I hesitate to judge individual differences as right
or wrong and my husband as a difficult person. Truth is,
we're both married to people who are difficult *at times.*

God's love in Christ overflows into our marriage so we
can make friends with our differences—and with each
other.

*Christ, my Savior, Your forgiveness changes every part of
my life! Thank You for a new heart and a new willingness to
honor my husband's individuality, to forgive, to be kind, and
even to be thankful that he is not like me.*

Try This: Think of one of your husband's traits that
you call difficult. Try to re-think it in less negative and
catastrophic terms.

The LORD God formed the man from the dust of the ground and breathed into his nostrils the breath of life, and the man became a living being. Genesis 2:7

The Breath of Life

If you're breathing, you have a 10-times-a-minute reminder of God's goodness!

Life was first breathed into Adam. Then Eve received her life from God through Adam.

On the cross, our sins took Jesus' breath away. *With a loud cry, Jesus breathed His last.*

And then God gave Jesus' breath back, the firstborn from the dead! His breath a guarantee that Jesus' work of salvation was completed.

Jesus breathed on His disciples at Pentecost, giving them the Holy Spirit.

And God still breathes on His people today! You are empowered for ministry by that same Holy Spirit breath of Jesus. As you breathe out the Good News, by the Holy Spirit's power people are convicted of sin and meet their Savior.

How graciously, and at what great cost, God fills you with the breath of life! What a privilege to share in God's work of salvation.

Creator God, every breath I draw reminds me of Your goodness! You've given me life, the gift of salvation, and the guarantee of eternal life. Thank You for the Holy Spirit, who breathes eternal life into those who hear the Word.

Try This: Sit quietly and observe your breathing. Thank God that you are alive to serve.

I will give you a new heart and put a new spirit in you; I will remove from you your heart of stone and give you a heart of flesh.
Ezekiel 36:26

More Precious than Raggedy Ann

When I was growing up, my mom made Raggedy Ann dolls. Stuffed with kapok, they were soft, floppy, winsome red-headed treasures.

There are Raggedy Ann Rules. Every doll has to have a red heart embroidered on her chest, hidden beneath her clothes.

You're more precious than Raggedy Ann because you have a *real* heart.

So He could replace your stone-cold heart with a warm living heart, Jesus died on the cross. It broke God's heart.

Now your heart reflects a new Spirit. Your heart washed clean in Baptism. Your heart refreshed and renewed in the Word and at the Lord's Table. Your heart made glad in Christian fellowship.

Sometimes you look a little raggedy because life is difficult. But even in the midst of a difficult life, your heart is alive in Jesus. Filled with God's love for the lost. Ready to be challenged to deeds of love.

Are you ready to wear your heart on your sleeve?

Thank You, Father, for replacing my stone-cold heart with a heart that's warm and committed to You and those You love. Forgive me when I behave in a cold-hearted manner. Show me how to display Your heart of salvation for all to see.

Try This: Make a little red heart and pin it under your clothes near your heart as a reminder that you no longer have a stone heart but a heart alive in Jesus.

Go and make disciples of all nations, ... I am with you always. Matthew 28:19–20

Would You Leave Ohio?

Muriel and Jasmine were pioneer sisters who left the comforts of Ohio for the rugged American West.

Women of raw courage, they were realists. They knew many did not survive illness, childbirth, or danger in the New West. They went anyway. Not fear*less*, but courageous in the face of fear.

Why did they leave Ohio?

Maybe Muriel's husband heard the call of the New Territory, so she packed. Maybe Jasmine craved adventure.

More likely, they were drawn by the vision of life in a new place, supported by the dream of working it out together, encouraged by fellow travelers.

Women in ministry are pioneers. Drawn by the vision of the Great Commission to tell people that their sins are forgiven in Christ. Supported by the faithfulness of the Great Commissioner. *As you go, I will be with you.*

God is with you on the ministry frontier. He supplies vision, courage, and fellow travelers.

For *that* vision, even you could leave Ohio!

Faithful Great Commissioner, keep Your vision of eternal life always before me. Thank You for Jesus who guarantees new life in Your presence forevermore! If necessary, make me willing to leave my comforts to serve You.

Try This: Remember when you felt irresistibly drawn by the vision and adventure of public ministry. Does it still seem like an adventure? If not, how can you recapture that spirit?

They sow the wind and reap the whirlwind.
Hosea 8:7

Follow the Recipe

Sometimes I spend the day in the kitchen. I like to cook. Most of the time.

Actually, I love to cook for special events but run out of enthusiasm for everyday mealtime.

I follow recipes the first time, usually improvise after that. Mostly make stuff up as I go.

God's recipe for blessed living is not make-it-up-as-you-go.

The Ten Commandments' wisdom and practicality come from God's infinite wisdom. Specific. Spare of words. Pointed. Given to bless us in godly living. To bless and make us a blessing.

They're not the Ten Suggestions.

Our age normalizes immorality, winks at thievery, makes right and wrong relative to how one *feels*.

And society is reaping the whirlwind.

Church workers claimed by the God of the Ten Commandments struggle to be obedient, to follow the recipe for blessed living. Because God commands it. Forgives your sins. Promises His Holy Spirit's help.

Under God's blessing, your obedience will attract people dizzied by the whirlwind.

Holy One, thank You for Jesus who obeyed the Ten Commandments perfectly in my place. Help me love Your recipe for godly living. Renew my desire to obey You in every circumstance. Make my obedience a witness in our godless society.

Try This: Read the Ten Commandments again (Exodus 20).

Unto you that fear My name shall the Sun of righteousness arise with healing in His wings.
Malachi 4:2 KJV

Shine Where You're Assigned

A missionary confronted a man with five wives. "You are violating God's Law," he said. "You must tell four of those women you are no longer their husband."

The man thought for a few moments then said, "Me wait here. You tell them."

Not every church worker is called to be the courageous, up-front leader.

Andrea is a principal, a clearly designated leader. She's comfortable with public accountability.

Lois is a faithful staff member. A detail person. She serves faithfully in the trenches. Responsible at the grass roots. A quiet leader behind the scenes. Lois gets the job done.

Whether you are instinctively a leader-chief or a leader-follower, God has given you a leadership bonus. Through your leadership, you get to introduce people to Jesus, the Sun of Righteousness who *has healing in His wings.* Healing for the sickness of sin.

Step up to leadership and reflect the Sun who heals.

Shine where you're assigned.

Sun of Righteousness, thank You for healing my sin-sick soul. I daily need the healing You bring. Show me how to lead in a way that reflects the brightness of salvation to everyone I am privileged to serve.

Try This: Think of a specific person who needs the healing of Jesus. Ask God to show you how your leadership might bring God's healing.

Each one should use whatever gift he has received to serve others. 1 Peter 4:10

Write a New Song

Irving Berlin lived to the age of 101, wrote nearly 1,000 songs, and never stopped composing.

He once said, "The question I ask myself is: *Are you going to be a crabby old man or are you going to write a new song?*"

God tells us that we have gifts for serving others. It's a fact.

Some scholars think the lists in 1 Corinthians and Romans 4 are not meant to be exhaustive but snapshots of God's marvelous generosity.

When you use and develop your gifts, your obedience can lead to the discovery of previously unknown gifts.

Someone advanced in years could still be *discovering new gifts from God.*

What an exciting thought!

That means you increase the variety of ways people can meet their Savior and Lord.

Be courageous. Experiment with new ministry methods. Offer to help in a ministry that requires skills you're not sure you have. Write a new song.

Invite God to surprise you.

Jesus, gift of God, thank You for saving me and equipping me for ministry. Please keep revealing Your ministry gifts and make me a useful tool in telling of Your redeeming love.

Try This: Is someone asking you to serve in an area you're afraid to try? Find a way to test your gift!

Isn't he the man who raised havoc in Jerusalem among those who call on this name? Acts 9:21

Former Hellion

Saul was a hellion. A troublemaker.

He had a reputation among the early Christians. When God told Ananias to heal Saul's blindness, Ananias argued. *Lord, I have heard many reports about this man and all the harm he has done.*

God insisted.

Ananias obeyed.

Saul was ready. He had been knocked to the ground by a bright light, seen and talked to the Lord Jesus, endured three days of blindness, not had any food or drink.

God used light to solve his Saul problem. Not by eliminating Saul, but by *illuminating* his mind and heart.

Maybe you've got a hellion, a child who has left the church and makes immoral or lawless choices. Someone who has quite a reputation in certain circles. And it breaks your heart.

God specializes in making *former* hellions. He paid dearly on the cross for their sins.

God turned Saul. He can turn your kid.

Don't give up. Pray for light from heaven!

God of hope, there is no problem too great for You. Thank You for dying on the cross so by Your grace, enemies of God become friends, hellions become former hellions. Renew my hope because of Your tender love and awesome power.

Try This: Read Acts 9 and keep praying.

It is hard for you to kick against the goads.
Acts 26:14

Kicking against the Goads

Sue and Eileen invite you to Ladies' Guild. A ho-hum afternoon.

Mrs. Thomason invites you to attend when your husband leads devotions at the seniors' dinner. Not a scintillating evening.

Vacation Bible school is just around the corner, and the leaders ask you to teach. You wanted to sew that week.

People keep asking, you keep sidestepping. Sometimes you grudgingly attend.

A goad is a sharp-pointed agricultural tool used to prod animals into action. While not pleasant, it does move stubborn, reluctant animals toward shelter or food or water.

Resistance brings misery, more pokes, unrest, dissatisfaction, more pokes, no peace. Jesus told Paul, *"You are hurting yourself by hitting back, like an ox kicking against its owner's stick."*

Invitations could be goads, nudging you into the life and ministry of your people. A resistive attitude only hurts yourself.

Maybe not guild, seniors, or VBS, but where *will* you serve? Actively move into some area of ministry. Every Christian can.

Good Shepherd, because of Your sacrifice on the cross, I am joined in ministry with my brothers and sisters. Show me where I can serve effectively. Make me willing to take the initiative and serve alongside Your people.

Try This: Before anyone asks, volunteer your service in an area that interests you.

71

Even in laughter the heart may ache.
Proverbs 14:13

Public Self

My husband and I had an argument. Make that a *big* argument.

I am sad. My eyes are red. I need some time alone.

Problem: The church potluck starts in less than an hour. Lots of people. Lots of people with needs. Kids and commotion.

Precisely the *last* place I want to go.

I repaired my face. Prayed. Then I gave my Public Self permission *not* to pretend the upper 20 percent of the feeling scale—happy, cheery feelings. No Academy Award performance.

My Public Self got to knock off the lower 20 percent too—those miserable, hopeless feelings. We have marriage work to do, and we're willing.

Ready for the potluck. Ready to be a real person with problems and needs like everyone there.

Not exactly Miss Cheerful but not the Princess of Gloom either.

Personally honest church workers make the wordless statement that Christ, our Savior, died for real people. People with problems and sins. What a powerful testimony!

God of truth, You are the very Truth that sets us free! Show us how to be free of the tyranny of public image so we can be authentic, truthful people who testify to Your redeeming love on the cross.

Try This: When you are tempted to pretend "the upper 20 percent," remind yourself that you can make an important faith statement by being authentically yourself.

He who has compassion on them will guide
them and lead them beside springs of water.
Isaiah 49:10

Follow Your Leader

Winston Churchill, Britain's prime minister when
morale was at its lowest, rose to the occasion brilliantly.

Following the Allied retreat at Dunkirk, Churchill
delivered his famous "We shall never surrender" speech.

Immensely popular in wartime, Churchill was
immensely *un*popular in peacetime. He was voted out of
office after the war.

Some people seem to be born leaders; some acquire
the skill.

You may not have Winston Churchill's charisma or his
talent for crisis management, but people still expect you
to lead.

The most important thing a church worker can do is
follow your Leader.

Your leader is the God of compassion. He knows your
strengths and weaknesses and has pledged to save you.

Your Leader leads you beside springs of water. Water
mixed with lifeblood that flowed from Jesus' side, the very
pledge that Jesus' work of salvation was finished. Sweet
baptismal water that refreshes the parched soul!

Follow your Leader so you can lead people to *their*
Leader.

*Water of Life, thank You for saving me in baptismal water
and refreshing me with living water. I am sorry for the times
I have failed to faithfully lead people to You. Refresh and
renew me so I will be an effective leader.*

Try This: Examine your leadership in light of the call
to be one who leads people to meet their Savior.

Do everything without complaining or arguing. Philippians 2:14

The Trouble with Harry

The trouble is that Harry's a pessimist. Harry complains.

Harry says the organ is too loud, the preaching inferior, and nobody takes their cranky kids to the nursery anymore. Harry complains that nonmembers use school scholarships. New members ablaze with enthusiasm and bright ideas are doused with Harry's cold water of complaint.

He wears me out. He wears me down. I complain about Harry!

Harry gets his power from people like me who take him too seriously. And *Harry's* not going to change.

I can change. I can inoculate myself against Harry's pessimism by expecting him to be consistent. Harry's going to complain. It's what Harry does. But we're getting on with the work of the church.

Give Harry a fair hearing. *Don't* wilt. Then matter-of-factly get back to work.

By God's grace, Harry and I are *fellow* redeemed, joined under the cross of Christ.

My calm leadership will enable us to get on with ministry.

Lord Jesus, You are the head of Your body the church. I confess that I complain and doubt Your wisdom when I must deal with difficult people. Thank You for forgiving my sin. Show me how to get on with the saving work of the church.

Try This: Pay attention to how much time and energy you squander complaining about people who make you crazy. Resolve to redirect that energy for ministry.

Let the morning bring me word of Your unfailing love, for I have put my trust in You.
Psalm 143:8

Love in Any Language

It was a convention breakfast. I sat down, smiled, said, "Good morning." Minimal response. Frankly puzzled looks. Some people aren't morning people, I guess.

I didn't get it.

Silence. I'd picked the only silent table in the whole room!

I still didn't get it.

Then I looked carefully at each woman. *I got it.*

These women were deaf. I had chosen the cafeteria table where deaf women were sitting together.

My love failed. I don't sign. Could we communicate?

So I ate and sneaked glances. They were absorbed in conversation, signing, laughing, making expressive faces. Talking as women everywhere do.

If my love had failed, God's hadn't.

One person asked me a question. The others waited with interest while she signed my answer. Soon we had caught the rhythm of conversation, hampered only by *my* disability.

God's unfailing love, having once crossed the barrier of sin to save and unite us, had now crossed the language barrier.

God of love, forgive me when I miss opportunities to share Your love because I am afraid of differences. Thank You for the unity You purchased by Your Son's death on the cross. Show me how to enjoy it in every situation.

Try This: Be aware of people who may feel like they're on the outside. Extend a welcoming hand.

Do not be afraid of people. Matthew 10:26 TEV

You Can Do It

Bible translator Bob Conrad was in trouble.

Traveling in Papua New Guinea, he underestimated the Amagu River current at flood stage. He tried to cross and was swept helplessly downstream.

Bob cried, "Lord, help me!" Benny Gabriel and three friends ran to save him. It was the first time anyone had gone down in the floodwaters of the Amagu and survived.

Church visitors might feel a bit like Conrad, swept away in the crowds and commotion of Sunday morning worship.

While we're busy catching up with friends and making committee contacts, visitors float unnoticed downstream and right out the door, never to be seen again.

Even if you're uncomfortable around strangers, say a silent, "Lord, help me!" rush over there, and extend your hand of welcome.

If Benny and his friends can risk their lives to rescue a stranger, you can risk social discomfort to rescue a visitor. His or her eternal life might depend on it.

Lord, Savior, Helper! Thank You for rescuing me from sin and certain death through Your atoning sacrifice. I am sorry for the many times I have ignored people You have sent to our church. Give me courage!

Try This: Next Sunday look around for a visitor and warmly extend God's welcome.

The LORD gave and the LORD has taken away;
may the name of the LORD be praised. Job 1:21

Life's Not Fair

Gerald Sittser's wife, daughter, and mother were killed in an accident.

He wrote in *The Christian Century:* "Perhaps I did not deserve their deaths; but I did not deserve their presence in my life, either.

"Living in a perfectly fair world appeals to me. But deeper reflection makes me wonder.

"In such a world I might not experience tragedy; but neither would I experience grace, especially the grace God gave me in the form of three wonderful people whom I lost."

Church workers often meet people who are angry that God would allow tragedies to occur to people who have lived good lives.

Sittser understands God's mercy in denying us fairness.

Because of sin, what we *deserve* is to be forsaken by God now and for eternity. In our place, Jesus experienced terrible desolation on the cross. Then He rose as victor.

By God's grace, we get what we *don't* deserve: eternal life and daily grace.

Life's not fair, thank God.

God of mercy, thank You for Your undeserved love in every area of my life. I am sorry that I sometimes complain about Your wisdom and mercy. Teach me to trust You.

Try This: Make a "Things I Don't Deserve" list and thank God for His goodness.

My Father will honor the one who serves Me.
John 12:26

First Lady of the Parish

It was after my husband's installation service and reception. We were mingling informally, trying to gracefully leave.

The kind older gentleman held both my hands warmly in his and said, "I say 'Welcome!' to the first lady of the parish!"

I probably said, "Thank you," but his words made me squirm. "First lady" has an unwelcome royal ring. I didn't want the responsibility.

We left seven years later, and I was grateful to have been their first lady.

They infrequently used the title, but I heard it as a sign of respect. I heard it as a recognition of my sacrifices. I also knew it was a way to honor my husband and his work.

Not an obligation, but a humbling trust.

Jesus promised, *My Father will honor the one who serves Me.* How generous of God—and how humbling it is—to receive the honor of God's people.

First lady of the parish. Undeserved grace. Again.

Lord, it is a privilege to serve You and Your people. Thank You for honoring my service, even though it is flawed and tainted by my sin and humanness. I don't deserve Jesus' love, but I humbly thank You for His redeeming sacrifice.

Try This: Practice positive paranoia—the belief that there are lots of people out there who love you and wish you well.

It has been granted to you on behalf of Christ not only to believe on Him, but also to suffer for Him. Philippians 1:29

Intrigued by Problems

Homer Neal reflected on his selection as interim president at the University of Michigan: He wouldn't baby-sit the university, but he would work to solve problems.

"I am intrigued by problems."

A church worker *intrigued* by problems? Yes, if she focuses on mission, not problems, so solving problems is what's necessary *to accomplish the mission.*

What about you?

You believe on Christ and are called to suffer for Him. Through God's gift of faith, you claim Christ's payment as full payment for your debt. You're free to focus on ministry. Even when it means suffering.

You're called to faith *and* suffering.

Ready to wade into problems that hamper Gospel ministry? Ready to deal with difficult people? Ready to occasionally have your inner peace disturbed? Ready to wrestle with complex issues?

The God who saved you for eternity has proven Himself trustworthy. *Wade into intriguing problems!*

My Savior, Christ, thank You for paying my debt so I am freed for ministry. Keep before me the mission of bringing Your saving love to the lost. Give me courage to tackle problems courageously—and even be intrigued and challenged by them.

Try This: If you're overwhelmed or scared by a problem, ask God to help you see your job in terms of the final goal: removing impediments to Gospel ministry.

He was despised and rejected by men, a man of sorrows, and familiar with suffering. Isaiah 53:3

Thou Shalt Not Whine

"We pick a president, then we pick on him," two-time Democratic presidential nominee Adlai Stevenson joked in the 1950s.

Do church workers get picked, then picked on?

Sometimes. It shouldn't surprise us.

Politicians like Stevenson *assume* people in the public arena will be targets of criticism and complaint. It comes with the territory.

But it shouldn't be that way in the church, you say?

Love fails everywhere. Even in the church.

Jesus was no stranger to failed love. Consider our Savior. Despised. Rejected. A man of sorrows. Stricken by God, pierced for our transgressions, crushed for our iniquities.

Jesus experienced failed love firsthand *and died because of it.* Now you'll never experience God's rejection or the absence of God's love.

Our sufferings don't compare. So suck it in. This is one part of life in public ministry. It may be unpleasant, but *it's not going to kill you.*

The one who was killed is alive and works beside you.

Lord Jesus, You experienced soul suffering on the cross, and God accepted Your suffering in place of mine. Make me willing to endure the difficulties and hurts of public ministry so many lost people will know Your saving love.

Try This: Read Isaiah 53 and marvel at Christ's suffering and death for you.

Show proper respect to everyone. 1 Peter 2:17

Good Manners Are Good Ministry

Good manners hardly inspire admiration these days.

Sadly, "It is for our faults that we are loved," opines Miss Manners. Ignorance of table manners denotes democracy—verbal roughness, honesty. Neglected thank-you notes signal self-important busyness. Picnic attire replaces Sunday best.

Should church workers care about good manners?

It's only fair to tell you I'm on the side of thank-you notes.

I think God is too. Thank-you notes demonstrate respect. A small, everyday reflection of the love God used to save us. They emphasize that we and our people bear the image of God.

A note of thanks speaks gratitude to an equally busy family who reserved time, planned, shopped, cooked, cleaned, incurred extra expense, and invested energy. Church workers aren't royalty who deserve all that.

It's a small gesture to pen a few words in appreciation.

If you have time to enjoy social favors, you have time to appreciate those favors.

Good manners are good ministry.

Almighty God, I am overwhelmed by the undeserved love and respect You afford me. Show me how to honor and respect others through everyday courtesies. Teach me to be consistent in my witness to Your love and regard for all people.

Try This: Read an etiquette book with an eye toward enhancing your ministry of respect.

The Pharisees and the teachers of the law muttered, "This man welcomes sinners and eats with them." Luke 15:2

The Mark of Your Ministry

It's not a pretty sight. Visitors show up at PTL or women's Bible study and no one welcomes them.

They've demonstrated courage to attend that first time. Courage and *hope*.

Meanwhile, we're comfortable and not *intentionally* rude.

Jesus had an eye out for people who didn't fit. Publicans. Sinners. Women. Even tax collectors. It was a mark of His ministry.

He welcomed them. Ate with them. Looked them in the eye. Wanted to know them.

Jesus knew that personal contact was how people could meet the God who had planned their salvation. Person to person. Savior to saved. A warm welcome into the kingdom.

They met the God of salvation face to face! He welcomed them.

As a church worker, you can help that happen for first-timers. Watch for them. Resolve that *there will be no unintentional rudeness here.*

You know how it feels to be the new person. Make a warm welcome the mark of your ministry.

God of salvation, thank You for welcoming me into the kingdom by baptismal water and the promise of Your Word. Bless my welcome to visitors with Your Holy Spirit's power that it may become the doorway to salvation.

Try This: If you don't know what to say to visitors, ask family and friends what helps them feel welcome and at ease in a new group.

There is now no condemnation for those who are in Christ Jesus. Romans 8:1

My Past Torments Me

Here I am, a professional church worker. I'm an example.

If they only knew.

I'm tormented by my past. Youthful sins. Deliberate disobedience. I've grieved God's heart.

People think I'm so good. They think that just because I love God and am committed to ministry, I must be kind of holy—and always have been.

If they only knew.

I know I'm not worthy of the respect they give me.

If they only knew.

God knows. And forgives. The Gospel you love to share has seared your heart with its hot coals of Law and refreshed your spirit with the water of life. When Christ died, the sins that grieve God and torment you were buried with Him.

There is now no condemnation. God accepted Christ's punishment as enough.

It was enough. God chooses to forgive *and* forget.

Actually, you're the perfect person to offer joyful, Gospel-centered ministry. You've experienced grace, amazing grace, firsthand.

Jesus, my Savior, thank You for Your grace and mercy to me, a convicted sinner. Help me grow in faith and the belief that my sins are forgiven and removed. Enlarge peace—a fruit of Your Spirit—within me.

Try This: When you are tormented by sins that are already forgiven, ask God to help you reject those thoughts and replace them with thanksgiving.

Stop Doing It

A cartoon shows Mark and Peg watching a televised marriage counselor. The counselor asks, "You know that *thing* you do to each other?"

Ah! They *know.* Cold shoulders. Sarcastic cracks. Nagging. Unkind humor. Little ways of getting even. Everyday domestic warfare.

Even in church workers' homes.

"Stop doing it!" the counselor shouts.

Of course, that simple wisdom isn't new. But it does go against our nature. It's difficult to see the part our natural self plays in our marriage problems.

So it's simple: You're to go against your nature and stop sinning.

Simple? Impossible! To make that happen, you'd need a whole new nature.

Thanks to God, you have one. When He died on the cross, Jesus grafted us into His new nature. He rose victorious, proving He had defeated the power behind your old nature. Christ's victory is yours.

By His Spirit's power, in daily vigilance, God will help you stop sinning—and commit to doing good. So stop doing that *thing.*

Victorious Savior, I am sorry when I act as if I have no choice about my behavior. Thank You for making change possible. Bless my commitment to doing good in my marriage.

Try This: Can you identify a *thing* you do in your marriage? Ask God to help you stop it.

If God gives a man wealth and property and
lets him enjoy them, he should be grateful
and enjoy what he has worked for. It is a gift
from God. Ecclesiastes 5:19 TEV

Life's Little Luxuries

Hot fudge sundaes—with pecans. A blue sky afternoon in the park with your kids. Dinner out, just the two
of you.

Life's little luxuries. Signs of God's goodness.

The writer of Ecclesiastes answers objections: Won't
life's pleasures distract us? Shouldn't we be saving it?
Maybe people will criticize.

The philosopher takes a look at life and its shortness,
notes the transitory nature of wealth, and concludes: *If
God gives you good things, be grateful and enjoy them. It will
keep your mind off how short life is.*

Maybe life's little luxuries are *supposed* to divert our
attention. Away from our worries and attempts to control
life. Onto God the giver.

The big things are under control. You have God's
priceless gift, your Savior, Jesus. Eternal life is yours. You
have peace with God.

Then God gives luxuries. A family vacation. A hike in
the woods. A great cup of coffee *and* time to enjoy it.

Savor all God's gifts!

*Generous God, giver of every good gift, I am sorry for the
times I disdain the wonderful surprises and luxuries You provide. Show me how to receive gratefully, acknowledging You.*

Try This: When you're tempted to bypass one of life's
little luxuries, decide instead to experience and savor it as
a gift from God.

I, Paul, write this greeting in my own hand.
Remember my chains. Colossians 4:18

Ministry in Word and Deed

A Ku Klux Klan supporter was being beaten by Klan protesters. Keshia Thomas threw herself on top of him, absorbing the blows.

"It was instinctive," she said. "I hope my actions speak powerfully against violence." Thomas is an African-American Christian.

She joins many Christians who have put their lives where their faith is.

Paul wrote from prison: *Remember my chains.*

Paul's chains—the visible reminder that he wasn't a fair-weather Christian enthusiast. Committed for life. Ready for death. Filled with the hope of heaven. Concerned that his life spoke as eloquently as his words. *Remember my chains.*

Christ's body bore the marks of sacrifice. *Look at My hands and My feet.* Flesh-and-blood proof that the resurrected Lord was the same Lord who suffered and died.

Committed to your salvation, His sacrifice made a new covenant with His Father. His resurrected body the pledge that God kept His word.

God uses you—in word and deed!

God of word and deed, thank You for speaking and accomplishing my salvation. Show me how to live my faith in unmistakable witness to Your faithfulness. Give me the instinct and the courage to put my faith into action.

Try This: Ask God to show you new ways to act on your faith.

So they are no longer two, but one. Matthew 19:6

The New Deal

An unhappy spouse penned this poem.

> When I got married I was looking for an ideal.
> Then it became an ordeal.
> Now I want a new deal.

The reality check is that marriage, for all its genuine delights, is still a life-long exercise in problem solving. No ideal people.

When you're married, *it's always something.*

This side of heaven, that's normal marriage, even for church workers.

But life without the ideal doesn't have to be an ordeal. There are great moments when we know the joy of God's wisdom in giving us to each other!

Enjoy the math of grace: One plus one *plus One* equals one. God mysteriously creates unity, causing two to become one in His presence.

The new deal is available *inside* marriage. God forgives you and makes you willing and able to forgive each other.

By God's grace and in His presence, you can work on problems and still enjoy unity.

Such a *new* deal!

God of unity, thank You for your mysterious oneness in my marriage. I am sorry for the times I have not nurtured the unity You give. Make me willing to forgive, even as You have forgiven me.

Try This: When you're dealing with a difficult marriage problem, deliberately affirm the unity God has given you.

Then all the disciples deserted Him and fled.
Matthew 26:56

Love under Pressure

"What's your perfume?" the nurse asked.

Of course I knew, but I couldn't name it until I held the bottle that night at home.

My memory failed because my husband was ill and I had been living and breathing *hospital* for weeks. Stressed and adrenaline-pumped.

Adrenaline temporarily unplugs the cerebral cortex, the brain's best thinking part. People under stress forget, think simplistically, and act impulsively.

The night He was arrested, Jesus' disciples pumped adrenaline. Chaos. Confusion. Peter cut off a man's ear. *All the disciples deserted Jesus and fled.*

Only Jesus was rational, insistent on His work of salvation.

Jesus invited Judas to do his deed, healed the ear, scolded Peter and those who would interrupt His plan. Jesus knew the suffering ahead. He was steady, grounded in His Father's love.

Maybe you pump adrenaline under the stress of public ministry. You can be steady if you're grounded in your Father's love and look to a Savior who knows your troubles.

God of grace, thank You for staying the course and accomplishing my salvation by Your death on the cross. Make me a steady, stable servant who is grounded in Your love and who looks to You for security and purpose.

Try This: When you're confused or forgetful, check your stress level and ask God to calm and steady you.

There on the poplars we hung our harps ... .
How can we sing the songs of the Lord while
in a foreign land? Psalm 137:2, 4

Sing the Lord's Song

They're so happy to meet you. Your heart is breaking as you smile and greet them. They're full of hope and expectation. You are too.

But there's still a gaping, raw wound. Your last ministry place and people are only a poignant good-bye away.

These people don't know what you've given up to be here.

This is a foreign land! How can you sing the songs of the Lord? By remembering they're songs *of the Lord.*

Songs of the Lord tell how God delivered His people from eternal death, a death that stranded Christ in a foreign land, apart from God.

Now you'll never be in a foreign land away from God. Even where you are now.

Though grieving, you can sing the Lord's salvation song to this people. And sing *with* them.

It's why you came when they called.

Go ahead and grieve. But remember, the place you left was also a foreign land when you arrived.

My Savior, Christ, thank You for singing the sweet song of salvation so it resonates in my soul. Thank You for caring about the pain I feel when we move. Show me how to sing Your salvation song, even when I feel sad.

Try This: Talk with your family about the sometimes confusing mixture of happy-sad feelings that accompany a move to a new ministry place.

God will speak to this people, to whom He said, "This is the resting place, let the weary rest"; ... but they would not listen.
Isaiah 28:11–12

Go Play

"Why don't you just drop everything some weekend and come up to our cabin?" she suggested as we walked out of church.

I fixed this dear, generous woman in an icy stare I'm still ashamed of and spit out, "My husband works weekends."

She was chagrined. I was angry.

Not angry with her. Angry that our personal choices, our commitment to public ministry, precluded and eliminated many opportunities for play.

As I look back on her offer, I think God was offering rest and *I would not listen.* I wish I had suggested a weekday.

Church workers who seldom play give a confusing witness.

God has created the universe, sacrificed His Son for your salvation, and sent His Holy Spirit to teach you how to live. He is Master of the universe and Lord of the church.

It's okay to leave your work at the church for a few hours. And go play.

Loving Father, I confess that I often have refused rest, thinking I can't relinquish for a moment the important kingdom work You've given me. Forgive me for Christ's sake. Teach me to trust You so my witness to Your sovereignty is credible.

Try This: Go play.

We continually remember before our God and
Father your work produced by faith, your
labor prompted by love, and your endurance
inspired by hope. 1 Thessalonians 1:3

Good-Mouthing

To win team gold in the 1996 Olympics, U.S. gymnast
Kerri Strug had to vault on an injured ankle.

In an unnerving, breathtaking, and dramatic climax,
Strug vaulted flawlessly.

The team won, the crowd went wild, and her grateful
teammates headed to the podium for gold medals. Medics
arrived to take Strug to the hospital.

Coach Bela Karolyi brushed everyone aside and carried Strug to the podium. Every step of the way, Karolyi
talked to Strug. *Listen to the cheers! You've worked so hard
for this! Listen to the cheers!*

Church workers also can help people hear the cheers:

- Women still talk about how great the retreat was.
  Tell Mildred.
- The guild loves the new banner closet Don made.
  Tell Don.
- It was a good PTL meeting. *Tell Nancy.*

St. Paul was an accomplished good-mouther, first
thanking God, then thanking and praising people.

Cheer. And help people hear the cheers.

*Christ, gift of God, thank You for my salvation and for
joining me with other redeemed brothers and sisters. Show
me how to encourage and build up Your people so they
abound in works of faith and serve You with great joy.*

Try This: For a month, pass on your own and others'
genuine praise. Evaluate the effects of good-mouthing.

They spew out swords from their lips ... . But I
will sing of Your strength. Psalm 59:7, 16

Swordtalk

Business research reports a happy customer will talk
about a pleasant experience for about 18 months and tell
five people.

An unhappy customer will remember the incident for
23.5 years and tell at least nine people—each of whom
will tell five others.

The defeated Old Adam lives! *Sigh.*

Church workers meet unhappy members who can list
their complaints alphabetically. Some, wronged by other
Christians, have broken hearts. Some have grievances that
seem petty and insubstantial—to us.

Many *spew out swords from their lips.*

You have no control over what disgruntled people say,
but you *can* help them work toward reconciliation and
peace.

Christ's death reconciles you to your Father, wraps
you in life, and gives you strength for courageous living.

God is in the reconciliation business and delights to
supply the personal strength and courage you'll need to
help swordtalkers become peacetalkers.

Swordtalkers are scary. Introduce them to the God
who can turn them into peacetalkers.

*Reconciling Father, thank You for receiving Christ's sacri-
fice in place of mine. I am sorry when I shrink from Your
work of reconciliation, especially when people are angry and
unpleasant. Enlarge Your Spirit's courage in me and so bless
Your people.*

Try This: Read a book about Christian conflict management.

92

"If I said something wrong," Jesus replied,
"testify as to what is wrong." John 18:23

When You're Mistreated

Annas asks illegal questions because the accused does not have to prove innocence. Accusers must prove guilt. When Jesus reminds the court of this, someone slaps His face.

Now a calm and resolute Jesus again challenges His accusers to obey the law.

Jesus is remarkably consistent. He was born to die for our sins. He's not lost His grip on His life's purpose: to help people meet and believe in their redeeming, loving God.

Jesus was never a helpless victim, a namby-pamby doormat who ignored disrespect. Before His death, He was clear about His active participation. *No one takes My life from Me, but I lay it down of My own accord.*

When you're mistreated, your ministry is on the line—threatened by your natural inclination to give up or act up.

Jesus did neither. Calm, respectful, courteous, He used existing rules and procedures.

When you're mistreated, do what Jesus did. Your ministry's integrity depends on it.

Friend of sinners, I am sorry that my attempts to defend myself often result in sin and invite others to sin too. Teach me to be calm and respectful so the ministry You have set before me is not compromised.

Try This: When you're mistreated, ask God to help you respond in a way that pleases Him.

Do not throw away your confidence; it will be richly rewarded. You need to persevere so that when you have done the will of God, you will receive what He has promised.
Hebrews 10:35–36

Don't Throw Away Your Confidence

He seemed a reasonable guy.

But as we worked to invent a special ministry for our congregation, Jim proved irrational and uncooperative.

He knew it wouldn't work. It wouldn't work *here*. It wouldn't work *unless* we did it his way.

His pessimism overwhelmed me. When I got home, I cried. Then I was angry and discouraged.

Life is short. Who needs this?

Through prayer and study, I knew this ministry was God's will.

So I got ready for Jim. Took notes when he objected. Did my homework. Brought solutions to the next meeting. Then new objections, new homework, new solutions.

The ministry took shape, details intensely scrutinized, problems excruciatingly anticipated. Now others joined with great excitement to plan and work for this ministry.

Jim's last words before we launched: *It will never work.*

It did work. Marvelously. Beyond our wildest expectations. Under God's will. By God's grace and blessing.

And because of Jim.

Lord God, You are Savior and Lord of the church. Help us discern Your call into difficult, challenging ministries and to deeply desire your will. Enable us to persevere so Your will can be accomplished, even through difficult people.

Try This: Learn from those who resist and annoy you.

When I want to do good, evil is right there
with me. ... Who will rescue me from this
body of death? Romans 7:21, 24

Can't Help Myself!

Charlie entered the pet shop. From the parrot's cage
he heard: *Hey, Buddy!* What? *You're ugly and your wife's
stupid!* Shocked and enraged, Charlie reprimanded the
parrot, who brazenly repeated the insults.

Charlie appealed to the shopkeeper, who scolded the
parrot. Blessed silence! Charlie headed for the door, satisfied.

Hey, Buddy! What? *You know what!*

The irresistible urge to insult. St. Paul knew about sinful impulses.

In Paul's day, murderers had their victim's corpse
lashed to their bodies—a foul, disgusting punishment.
Paul calls his urge to sin a corpse, a body of death.

Who will rescue me?

There's good news: You've been rescued!

Because of sin, you were permanently joined to
death—and destined to carry death into eternity. Christ
took that repulsive body of death and carried it Himself,
its weight crushing Him. Then He rose victorious, Lord of
death.

Now you have impulse control, a sign of new life. By
His Spirit's power, you can resist the irresistible.

*Lord of life and death, thank You for rescuing me from
irresistible sin, a pungent body of death! By Your Holy Spirit, increase my willingness to say no to familiar sins so my life
will please You.*

Try This: Identify a familiar sin and ask God to show
you how to resist.

For Christ died for sins once for all, the righteous for the unrighteous, to bring you to God.
1 Peter 3:18

Bring People to God

A plane falls from the sky. Thousands grieve.

Floods destroy a community. Families are homeless.

A terrorist bomb explodes, killing eight teenagers. Their families will never fully recover.

Daily news, tragedies, bombs, disasters, lawlessness. Is there a *Christian* way to manage the news?

For every person in today's news, Christ's death was full payment for sin. Most don't know they're loved and redeemed.

The daily news provides a unique opportunity to bring people to God in prayer.

Raise people to God in prayer, praying that the lost will meet their Savior and that Christians will not give up the faith and become bitter. Pray for healing. Pray for repentance. Thank God for a 50th wedding anniversary. Pray for reconciliation. Pray for godly leaders.

When you regard news stories as news of people God loves, those stories will trickle into your prayer life—and into worship services, devotions, prayer chains, small groups.

Bring people to God for prayer.

Christ, refuge from the storms of life, I confess that I am at times indifferent to the troubles of others. Fill me with compassion for these people You have redeemed with Your most precious blood.

Try This: Choose one story from today's news and pray for the people involved.

Be strong and courageous, and do the work.
Do not be afraid or discouraged, for the LORD
God, my God, is with you. 1 Chronicles 28:20

Don't Be Discouraged

Deaconess Helen is thinking of becoming a song-writer. Cowboy songs.

She's going to write a sequel to the refrain: *Where seldom is heard a discouraging word And skies are not cloudy all day.*

Life on Helen's particular range has plenty of discouraging words and lots of clouds. And complaints. And problems.

She's wondering if she's got the wrong job. Maybe she should *be* a cowgirl, not just write about them.

Escape fantasies help. Short term.

For the long term, the only thing that will help and encourage you is believing God's faithfulness. Breathing in God's faithfulness. Wrapping it around you like a blanket.

The Lord God knows and forgives your sins. He's set ministry before you. He trusts you to tell your people their sins are forgiven.

Be strong and *en*couraged as the Lord God stands with you at cloudy, discouraging times. Remember your salvation, embrace your call to ministry, immunize yourself against the grumbling, and *do the work.*

Faithful Savior and Lord, thank You for calling me to ministry here, now. Thank You for faithfully standing next to me on cloudy and sunny days. Fill me with courage and enthusiasm for the ministry before me.

Try This: Modify an old song so the words give you a laugh and encourage you.

Practice hospitality. Romans 12:13

We'll Keep the Light on for Ya

Many people *assume* every church worker's wife has the spiritual gift of hospitality. I don't have that gift.

Some church workers welcome people into their homes as if they were train stations. I like privacy.

Don't get me wrong. I not only entertain members, church staff, elders, friends, relatives, and lots of other folks, *I enjoy it.*

Nevertheless, hospitality is not my natural inclination so I am deliberate and disciplined.

I'm in training. And I practice.

Good manners show respect so I've learned about etiquette. I pay attention to details so people will be comfortable and enjoy themselves. I'm learning gracious ways to welcome strangers and newcomers at church.

Even if open-door hospitality isn't a natural for me, welcoming people God loves is a privilege.

Best of all, my warm welcome and open door could be the way someone will meet Jesus, the Open Door. God might use me to welcome them to heaven.

Welcoming, warmhearted Father! Thank You for welcoming me to heaven because of Jesus. I am sorry for the times I have been ungracious and inhospitable. Teach me how to be an ambassador of Your grace.

Try This: If you do not have the spiritual gift of hospitality, plan to learn some of the skills involved in offering hospitality.

I am among you as one who serves. Luke
22:27

It's Amazing!

*It's amazing what can be accomplished if you don't care
who gets the credit,* Emily thought.

This was a good VBS. More kids, more nonmembers.
More volunteers. A fresh spirit.

A far cry from last year.

Last year Emily hated VBS. It was an exhausting series
of turf wars and hurt feelings. And no snacks one day
because the snack lady quit in a huff.

A far cry from Jesus' service.

On the night He was betrayed, Jesus witnessed a dispute among the disciples.

Imagine! A dispute about who was the greatest, after
Jesus had said *My body given for you. My blood poured out
for you.* His terrible suffering the wages of our sin. His
very life the price of salvation.

Church workers can be able guerrilla fighters, losing
the war for souls to win turf and recognition.

Imitate Christ's servant leadership and set your heart
on ministry. It's an amazing model for the people you
lead.

*Christ, my servant leader, I confess that I have at times
traded ministry for recognition and turf. By Your Spirit's
power, make me a humble servant, clearly focused on ministry, a model for Your people.*

Try This: This week, systematically pray for everyone who works and volunteers at your church or school.

Each one of you also must love his wife as he loves himself, and the wife must respect her husband. Ephesians 5:33

I'm Always the Heavy

It's a church worker *system.*

He overworks, and you quietly suffer, take up the slack, pacify the kids, and make it work. And smile.

There's always one more needy person. One more crisis.

Then you blow. Up in anger, inward in depression, outward at unfortunates nearby. So he takes time off, pays attention, admits he needs to be home more.

But his resolve erodes, and he's back to overworking and you're back to suffering.

It's a *system,* an orderly process with a predictable outcome. Your anger and frustration trigger his behavior changes.

It's expensive in terms of love and respect. It debits your marriage, impacts your kids.

You need a new system. A system where you're not the heavy and he decides his behavior changes. A system rooted in God's Word and prayer, assisted by a professional counselor, permeated by forgiveness and God's promise to sustain and strengthen your marriage.

You don't have to be the heavy.

Christ, my Savior, You paid with Your life to make it possible for my husband and me to live in forgiveness. Thank You for the hope that brings to our marriage!

Try This: If you need to talk with a professional counselor, do it.

The LORD Almighty is with us; the God of
Jacob is our fortress. Psalm 46:7

How Can I Compete with God?

Peggy was distraught.

"It seems selfish to complain about my husband's long hours. He's doing God's work. How can I compete with God?"

The answer is simple: You can't compete with God because God hasn't entered a contest with you.

While overworking church workers may sincerely believe God is asking for every waking moment, it's a misperception.

God doesn't set up double binds, demanding two mutually exclusive, incompatible behaviors at the same time. The God who puts us in marriages and families wouldn't demand that all energies be spent at work.

So what's going on here?

This side of heaven, there are no pure motives. We choose work styles and family styles for complex, intriguing reasons, including family-of-origin patterns, personal fears, and sincere faith commitments.

God, who offered up His Son, doesn't want spouses and families sacrificed on church work altars. Rather, God wants to bless your marriage and family as you identify and work with your complex motivations.

God of truth, I am sometimes afraid to look at the complicated issues in my life. I trust You for my salvation because the Holy Spirit has given me faith. Show me how to trust You for the hidden truths in my marriage and family life.

Try This: Refuse to blame God for personal choices.

101

Am I now trying to win the approval of men,
or of God? Galatians 1:10

Invitation to Idolatry

Five-year-old Lisa told her enlightened '90s mom she wanted to be a nurse.

"A nurse! Lisa, just because you're female doesn't mean you have to be a nurse. You can be a surgeon, lawyer, banker, even president of the United States. You can be anything!"

"Anything?" Lisa asked. Her face lit up. "Okay, I'll be a horse!"

Wives of church professionals and women in church work used to inhabit a closed little world. Roles were rigid, expectations high, role transgressions severely punished.

Things have changed. Now you can be the person God had in mind when He made you uniquely you.

In one sense, rigid role expectations invite idolatry. Women can become fixed on winning approval and avoiding disapproval.

Softer role expectations invite greater accountability to *God*.

Under God's grace and bounty, you can serve Him in many roles: wife, mom, teacher, musician, encourager, nurse, follower, leader, to name a few.

But probably not *horse*.

Christ, my Savior, Your redeeming love gives my life purpose and meaning. Thank You for calling me to faith and equipping me to serve. Teach me to care most about what You think of me.

Try This: Talk with other ministry women about how role expectations have changed over the years.

102

God is faithful; He will not let you be tempted
beyond what you can bear. 1 Corinthians 10:13

It Must Be Wonderful to Be Married to Him!

"It must be wonderful to be married to him!" Talitha
gushed. "You're so lucky!"

Actually, *he's lucky to be married to me.* After all, he's
usually late for dinner, cuts up the newspaper before I've
read it, and wastes postage stamps on sweepstakes
entries.

Perfect he's not.

I just smile and nod when women deify him. They
intend a compliment. I've learned to be amused.

It only becomes a problem if he believes his press clip-
pings. Or if she compares her exalted ideal with her
imperfect husband. Or if I react by recounting his faults.

Public ministry is fraught with hidden dangers, unexpected opportunities for sin.

Even as Christ's death covers your sin and saves you
from its power, God protects you from temptations that
can ruin home and ministry.

So pray for your husband's humility, Talitha's marriage, and a sense of humor. And practice that smile and
nod.

Most days it *is* wonderful to be married to him!

*God, my Protector, thank You for the privilege and power
of prayer that puts a wall of protection around me and my
family. By faith I look to You for all I need to resist temptation.*

Try This: Start a collection of church worker cartoons.

If anyone is ashamed of Me and My word in this adulterous and sinful generation, the Son of Man will be ashamed of him when He comes in His Father's glory with the holy angels. Mark 8:38

Truth in Advertising

In the magazine *SoulCafe,* Len Sweet wondered, "Why can't the church write copy that makes being a disciple of Jesus as exciting and adventurous as driving a Mustang?"

I'll venture a guess.

Christians, church workers too, are afraid of being parodied as born-again fanatics. Afraid of violating political correctness. Afraid of disapproval.

I don't know personally a single person who has gone to jail for her faith. I don't know anyone who has been persecuted for his Christianity.

We're afraid of the wrong thing.

We ought to be afraid that people will be lost for eternity because they don't know their Redeemer. We ought to be afraid to leave the false impression that life with the Sovereign Lord lacks adventure and passion.

Tell the truth in this adulterous and sinful generation: Life with God beats driving a Mustang any day!

Saving Lord, I am sorry for being so afraid that I short-change and water down the tremendous impact of Your power to save. I claim Your promise of Your Holy Spirit's power to witness with enthusiasm and energy.

Try This: Think of a new and appealing way to describe your life with God.

Eubulus greets you, and so do Pudens, Linus, Claudia and all the brothers. 2 Timothy 4:21

Stress Fractures

"My husband and I are best friends."

I often hear that from church workers whose marriages are in trouble.

They entered public ministry as friends and teammates, a beautiful demonstration of faith and unity. But lack of time and social isolation work against healthy marriages.

Caught in the predictable church worker time crunch and socially isolated by the church worker mystique, couples may become mutually dependent and look *exclusively* to the other to meet personal needs.

Under the weight of that unrealistic demand, the relationship shows stress fractures: anger, disappointment, escalating demands.

Your husband can't possibly meet all your needs, just as you can't meet all of his. That's why God has joined you to Himself in Christ—and peopled your world with coworkers, relatives, neighbors, potential friends.

Go ahead, be best friends with your husband. God's gift! Then, like St. Paul, develop a life rich in spirit and mutually supportive relationships. And be glad when your husband does the same.

Jesus, friend of sinners, thank You for paying with Your lifeblood to make me a friend of God. Show me how to be a faithful and loving friend to my husband and the others You have put in my life.

Try This: Look for a friend in your neighborhood or community.

We have this hope as an anchor for the soul,
firm and secure. Hebrews 6:19

An Anchor for the Soul

I turned off the light and settled next to my sleeping husband.

I'm so glad this day is over.

What a terrible, awful, no good, very bad day.

Let me count the ways: Today I reaped the harvest of my own and others' sin; dealt uncharitably with a difficult person; missed a great chance to share God's love because I wasn't paying attention; said a stupid, thoughtless thing that hurt a friend's feelings. *And that was the morning.*

Then, as my day disintegrated, I struggled to regain control. And made everything worse.

In repentance, I survey the wreckage and look with hope to Christ, my Savior, who covers me with His coat of righteousness so I appear whole and unblemished before God. We both know what's under that coat, but God chooses to see only Christ's righteousness.

The sure hope of salvation is the anchor that secures my soul. God's grace invites me to live tomorrow graciously.

Jesus, hope of sinners! I am sorry for the utter creativity of my sinfulness. By faith I embrace Your forgiveness and thank You for Your gift of hope.

Try This: If the day disintegrates around you, S.T.O.P. and take a Spiritual Time Out for Prayer.

If anyone will not welcome you or listen to your words, shake the dust off your feet when you leave. Matthew 10:14

Romancing Resisters

Jesus was a realist.

When He sent the Twelve, He knew some people would resist salvation—even after the Twelve raised the dead, healed the sick, and drove out demons!

Jesus sent them anyway.

He also sends you into a resistive world and church.

It's called the Rule of 20–50–30: 20 percent of people are friendly to change, 50 percent sit on the fence, a noisy 30 percent actively resist.

Maybe you spend inordinate amounts of time and energy trying to romance that 30 percent into compliance.

Jesus didn't do that. *Die* for God's enemies? Absolutely! Yet He told the Twelve to shake off the dust. It's a balance to the long-suffering, patient lifestyle also asked of Christians.

There's a time to romance resisters and a time to shake off the dust. A time to pray and wait and a time to forge ahead.

It's not either/or. It's knowing *when*.

The Gospel message is urgent.

Go. Preach. Do not be afraid. Ask God for wisdom.

Lord, You desire the salvation of all people. Thank You for calling me Your own in Baptism and giving me ministry here. Fill me with love and wisdom so I know how best to serve those who resist.

Try This: Don't be surprised by resistance.

When Jesus saw him lying there and learned that he had been in this condition for a long time, He asked him, "Do you want to get well?" John 5:6

Helper's Rule Number 1

The Murphys had so many needs. Unchurched, destitute, Dad missing, Mom sick, kids in trouble. It was easy to take over. You liked helping.

Then their demands and calls escalated.

Compassion fatigue spread like chicken pox.

After spewing harsh words, the Murphys went to another church. You were hurt, disappointed, confused. What happened?

Maybe you broke Helper's Rule Number 1: Don't do for people what they can do for themselves.

If you take over responsibilities that rightly belong to others, you're out of order. Out of God's order that holds each person accountable for his or her own life.

People have a love-hate thing about being dependent. Helpers who overstep are rewarded with anger.

Jesus asked the invalid, *Do you want to get well?* to reveal the man's determination to take responsibility for his life after his healing.

Help people meet their own needs. Don't appropriate. It's Helper's Rule Number 1.

Lord, I've often asked You to take my responsibilities, but You always help me meet them myself. Thank You for saving me from the ruin of sin, doing what I could not do for myself.

Try This: Allow people to participate as much as they can in their own rescue.

I sought the LORD and He answered me; He delivered me from all my fears. Psalm 34:4

Teens Put Mileage on Your Faith

Margaret told Jill to slow down and enjoy her teen years. "Youth comes just once."

"Thank goodness!" Jill said. "I couldn't stand this abuse for a whole lifetime!"

Abuse? Hardly. She's loved and well cared for, just like your kids. But she speaks the teen perspective.

Unique *and* obsessed with conformity. Friends with green hair and nose rings. Danger and paganism in the air they breathe, the water they drink. Add the pressure of being *on view*, a church worker's kid. It's a formidable mix.

God knows the danger, and God loves your kid. When baptismal waters cascaded over her, God worked a miracle. He claimed her as His own for eternity and gave her the gift of faith. Even if she becomes a purple-haired teen, the promise and the gift are sure. God's commitment is a lifeline to teens and their parents.

Remember her baptism and God's dependability.

And hang on for a ride that'll put mileage on your faith.

Faithful God, thank You for the saving grace of my Baptism. Thank You for claiming my children as Your own and protecting them. Teach me how to be a godly parent in these difficult and confusing times.

Try This: Ask Christian parents of grown children how God helped them.

From the fruit of his lips a man is filled with good things as surely as the work of his hands rewards him. Proverbs 12:14

Time and a Half

The cartoon shows applicant J. L. Klutzenheimer standing in front of the seminary registrar's desk. "Do we get time and a half for working Sundays?" he asks.

You undoubtedly had more of a clue than poor Klutzenheimer, but maybe you didn't know what it would *really* be like to be a professional church worker or married to one.

In His goodness, God has loaded church work with delights. Time-and-a-half rewards. For instance:

- The privilege of introducing people to Christ, who bought their salvation and freedom from the power of sin.
- The awe of that golden moment when the Holy Spirit moves knowledge of salvation from head to heart—and saving faith is *there.*
- The joy of mining the Word, gleaning comfort and direction for complex lives.
- The privilege of serving people at the great milestones of Christian life, teaching the faith, shaping character.

God rewards the fruit of your lips with a rich harvest of faith and growth in righteousness.

Time and a half? *Better!*

Lord God, thank You for calling me into Your kingdom through my Baptism and giving me the Holy Spirit to direct my life. Thank You for the many privileges of public ministry. Keep me mindful of the eternal consequences of this work.

Try This: Thank God for blessing the labor of your lips.

Go home to your family and tell them how much the Lord has done for you, and how He has had mercy on you. Mark 5:19

All in the Family?

Meteorologist Stephen Lord's wife didn't believe him when he said, "The big one's coming!"

"She takes my prognostications with a grain of salt," admits Lord, a hurricane specialist. He finally persuaded her, and "in the end, she was glad."

Families of church workers may have similar problems being receptive to spiritual guidance and direction. Some pastors' wives lament, "I don't have a pastor."

In the social sciences, that conflict is called a *dual relationship:* One role or relationship hinders the other.

Actually, no matter what your husband does for a living, as a Christian he's to serve his family with the Gospel and provide God-pleasing leadership.

The challenge is to acknowledge the limitations of dual relationships with grace, not rancor. Agree it's okay to seek necessary spiritual care—and perhaps *provide* it for other church worker families.

God's Son died to have every member of your family in heaven with Him. *Do what it takes to stay spiritually healthy.*

Father, thank You for making us a family and sending Jesus to secure eternal life with You. I am sorry for the times I have neglected my spiritual health. Show me how to take appropriate responsibility for the nurture of my faith.

Try This: What spiritual need is not being met? What will you do about it?

Trust in the LORD and do good. Psalm 37:3

People Will Talk

"She's kind of like an appendage," explained a long-time observer of Houston's upscale social scene. "They're a very close couple."

Less than a month after her husband was elected Houston's mayor, Elyse Lanier was criticized for her decorating, faulted for not championing minority affairs, and censured for planning a city beautification campaign.

Called "Mrs. Mayor" and "Mayorette," she admitted dismay. "Everybody's got something to say about what I do."

Mrs. Lanier moved from private to public life. And forgot to take a deep breath.

Mrs. Pastor. Mrs. Principal. Mrs. Music. Sound familiar?

People will talk.

The psalmist has good advice: *Trust in the Lord and do good.*

It's what Jesus did.

People criticized, commented, harassed, and baited Him. He trusted His Father and His Father's will. And the good He did saved you from being forever separated from God!

Do good. Get on with the work set before you. Trust God to bless and protect you.

Lord of life, thank You for being immovable in Your resolve to help and save me. Show me how to live graciously with people's interest and opinions about my life and work. Make my life a loving witness to Your salvation.

Try This: Expect people to talk.

Suppose a man comes into your meeting
wearing a gold ring and fine clothes, and a
poor man in shabby clothes also comes in.
James 2:2

Where's Ralph?

Ralph was telling his story. Husband, father, prison guard.

Hates social stuff. Drives a cab to make ends meet.

Got interested in religion, started reading the Bible, then found a church where he could sit in the last pew, next to the old books and Bibles. The only pew without a cushion.

"Last week I was late. I went to my pew and sang the hymn. When it was time to sit down for the Bible lesson, it felt funny. *Somebody had fixed a cushion for my pew!*"

Hooray for Ralph's church! They're paying attention.

Ralph likes to be left alone. How do you reach a guy like Ralph?

By simple, thoughtful deeds that show respect.

Jesus was good at personalizing ministry. He paid attention to people and detail. His death on the cross was His personal sacrifice for you.

Look around. There's a Ralph out there to love and serve.

Jesus, my Savior, I am sorry for the times that I have missed opportunities to love and serve Your people in unique, personal ways. Teach me to love in the same way You love me: with compassion, thoughtfulness, and attention to detail.

Try This: Know someone who doesn't quite fit? Find a special way to serve her.

The LORD will hear when I call to Him. Psalm 4:3

The Invisible Line

My friend Shirley phoned, upset that her baby was *still* crying. Once there, I found two new teeth forcing their way through Hillary's gums. Shirley was thrilled. "Just wait till I say my pastor's wife found Hillary's first teeth!"

I was speechless. I thought we were *friends*.

It was a painful revelation: An invisible line separated us. Her friend was also her pastor's wife.

Actually, the invisible line has *two* sides. I seldom share intimate personal matters with member friends. It's hard for them to separate person and role. My idiosyncrasies or sins could become a hindrance to ministry.

Behind the-line-that-no-one-sees-but-everyone-honors, it's lonely.

Jesus cares how you feel. His blood covers sins and lines so *you are never alone.*

He gives unexpected opportunities to be friends with people who know you first as person, incidentally as church worker.

There are people for whom invisible lines are truly invisible. *Find them.*

Lord, You know how lonely I feel sometimes, disheartened by being set apart as a church worker. Make me aware of the unique ministry opportunities my position affords. Thank You for people who are able to see me apart from my work.

Try This: Don't be surprised when people see you as your role.

I will refresh the weary and satisfy the faint.
Jeremiah 31:25

Don't Start Packing

In 1849, Nathaniel Hawthorne was dismissed from his government job in the customs house. He went home in despair.

His wife listened to his tale of woe, set out pen and ink, lit the fire. Then she put her arms around him and said, "Now you will be able to write your novel."

Hawthorne wrote *The Scarlet Letter.*

Is there life after a rugged voters' meeting, a contentious board of education salary review, an encounter with an angry member?

A wife is usually the first sounding board, the first to hear the tale of woe. *You can be the first to share hope.*

Hope comes from believing God's promises. And God's promises find their yes! in Jesus who endured the cross and hell to purchase forgiveness of sins and life with God in heaven for you.

Jesus gives you hope in tough times.

So resist the urge to start packing. Put your arms around him. And speak hope.

Jesus, my hope, thank You for the gift of heaven and eternal security. Help me trust You in the midst of the troubles and insecurities of public ministry so I can speak hope to my husband and family.

Try This: Search the Bible for God's promises.

In love He predestined us to be adopted as His sons through Jesus Christ. Ephesians 1:4–5

Love to Spare

Tonya was nearsighted, klutzy. She usually forgot her homework and came to school without a bath.

Her classmates responded with indifference so this small, quiet child spent recess doing classroom jobs and shyly talking with Mrs. Bates.

One night Mrs. Bates read in the newspaper that Tonya's brother had been murdered. Big family trouble. State agencies stepping in.

The next day, at the school's annual hearing tests, the students wore headphones while Mrs. Bates whispered a sentence the students were to repeat aloud. *Washington was our first president. Lincoln lived in Illinois.*

When Tonya put on the headphones, Mrs. Bates whispered, *I wish you were my little girl.*

Church workers and their families have great opportunities to pay attention to kids in trouble—and mobilize others to love and affirm needy kids.

God graciously adopts you as His daughter and gives you the blessed inheritance—eternal life.

There's love to spare, so pass it on—to the Tonyas and Tonys.

God of mercy, it is by Your grace that I have saving faith and am joined with You for eternity. Thank You for graciously adopting me into Your forever family. Make me aware of children who need to know Your love and mine.

Try This: Look again at an awkward, neglected child. Ask God what to do.

Peacemakers who sow in peace raise a harvest of righteousness. James 3:18

Find Another Way

Quire Bruen was an English Puritan. At a dinner party, the host toasted the prince.

As the cup of wine was passed, everyone looked to see what the nondrinking Puritan would do.

He took the cup and said, "You may drink to his health, and I will pray for his health!" And passed the cup.

Bruen's genius was his flexibility, his ability to *find* another way.

Great church workers have great dreams of ministries and projects. Sometimes those dreams are specific, detailed.

Your job is to educate, work with people, help them understand and adopt the dream.

If you do it right, they'll have their own ideas and dreams. That will challenge your flexibility, invite you to acknowledge that most goals can be accomplished in more than one way.

The peace that Christ purchased on the cross is too precious to sacrifice on the altar of inflexibility. With grace, selflessness, and the Holy Spirit's power, *find another way.*

Christ, my Peace, thank You for Your death on the cross that brought peace with God and the freedom to be creative and interactive as I work with other Christians. Show me how to be flexible and innovative.

Try This: Read a book on creative problem solving.

And so you will plunder the Egyptians.
Exodus 3:22

Plunder the Egyptians

Barry is an embattled church worker who won't go to a counselor unless the counselor is a Christian. So his stress keeps mounting.

Patty wants Christian books about managing their limited church worker finances. She's stuck.

Before the children of Israel left Egypt, God said, *Ask the Egyptians for gold and silver and clothes.*

When the Israelites asked, the Egyptians gave. And the Israelites took it all with them, plundering the Egyptians.

Even as God met the Israelites' physical needs by plundering the Egyptians, so God gives us spiritual riches by sending Christ to cover our sins.

And if you're willing to pray for direction and trust God to help you evaluate, riches also await you in the non-Christian world.

A prayerfully sought, competent counselor will honor a couple's faith and values as a professional ethic. Good money managers help families incorporate faith commitments such as tithing.

A wealth of resources awaits prayerful, careful Christians.

Plunder the Egyptians.

Lord, You know what I need before I do. Thank You for loving and claiming me by Christ's sacrifice. I trust You for discernment and wisdom as I use the resources available to me in the world outside the church.

Try This: Every day this week, ask God to open your eyes to resources you need.

May the God of hope fill you with all joy and peace as you trust in Him. Romans 15:13

My Husband Doesn't Overwork

Here comes another overworking-pastor story!

A pastor's wife took her overworked husband to the family doctor. The doctor took her aside and whispered: "I don't like the way your husband looks."

"I don't either," she replied, "but he's always been a good father to the children."

For many, the words "overworked" and "pastor" are inseparably linked. But maybe you're married to a man who *doesn't* overwork and *isn't* beleaguered.

Perhaps your husband works *less* than he should, misses deadlines, doesn't prepare well. He doesn't stress himself, doesn't consider himself accountable.

In your heart of hearts, you know his critics are right. You're insecure, anxious, embarrassed, angry.

What to do? Pray for your husband and his work. Allow the natural, logical consequences of his behavior. Talk with a professional counselor about your feelings. Look to Christ and claim new life because He died for you. *And the God of hope will fill you with joy and peace.*

Christ, my hope, You are my strength and security. Thank You for saving me and sending Your Holy Spirit to enlarge my faith and help me trust in You. Show me effective ways to deal with my problems and new ways to love my husband.

Try This: If you usually rescue your husband from the consequences of his choices, stop.

Make it your ambition to lead a quiet life.
1 Thessalonians 4:11

Never Satisfied

Moshe Waldocks tells about a Jewish grandmother who took her grandson to the beach and fell asleep. She woke up to see her grandson flailing in the ocean, going down for the third time.

She prayed, "Creator of the universe, save my child, and I'll return to the righteous path!"

The boy was deposited alive on shore. She ran over, looked around, scowled, shook her finger at heaven. *"But he had a hat!"*

Some people are never satisfied. Some problems don't get solved. Some differences are irreconcilable. *Ah, life!*

It's true in your family-of-origin, your marriage, your church, all relationships this side of heaven. Imperfection runs rampant.

How can you *lead a quiet life* when the people in your life aren't perfect?

By trusting God for inner quiet, the deep peace that comes from being redeemed by Christ and comforted by God's Holy Spirit.

So don't come unglued around difficult, imperfect people. Some days *you're* the difficult one.

Lord, You are my quiet and rest in the middle of a difficult and imperfect world. By faith I claim the peace You won for me on Calvary. Let my quietness be a witness to Your presence in my life.

Try This: Don't be dismayed that some problems never get solved.

Be kind and compassionate to one another.
Ephesians 4:32

A Gesture of Love

Jim and Kelli haven't been married very long, but they're having that same argument again.

This time they're *finally getting somewhere.* A new understanding, an agreement about behavior changes.

The argument's over, but Jim and Kelli are both stirred up from the effort to communicate, the adrenaline rush, the ever-present fear of conflict. Something feels unfinished, and they can't get back to normal right away.

So Jim ambles out to the kitchen and calls to Kelli, "Want a root beer, honey?"

Her favorite soft drink. A small gesture of love.

It's a good way to end a fight. A good way to say, *We have a future together, and I'm glad.*

Because of sin, you were separated from God forever. But God has pledged you a future with Him in heaven, a pledge written in the blood of His Son. An enormous, breathtaking sign of His love!

Next fight, end with a sign of hope, a small gesture of love.

Dear God, because of Your love, we have a future together, and I'm glad! Thank You for the gift and hope Your salvation brings to my heart and my marriage. Give me the grace to reach out after an argument with a sign of love and hope.

Try This: Think of one small, ordinary gesture that would speak hope to your husband.

Search me, O God, and know my heart ... . See if there is any offensive way in me. Psalm 139:23–24

The Power of an Apology

"In my early years of ministry, I refuted people who said I had offended them or hurt their feelings. I'd say, *I'm sorry you took it wrong.* But then they'd write again, doubly hurt because I implied they were hypersensitive.

"Now I write, *Thank you for expressing your hurt. I'm sorry. Please forgive me,* and people say how much my apology means to them.

"Our people already know we make mistakes. They want to know if we have the integrity to admit them" (Bill Hybels, *Leadership Magazine*).

As a church worker, your mistakes may be exposed and magnified by the spotlight of public scrutiny. That's why ordinary mistakes can seem like cataclysmic disasters.

But God can use public mistakes to prove your witness: Will you admit that you are a fallen sinner and depend on God's forgiveness? Will you apologize and accept responsibility? Will you live and respond to sin in your life as if the Gospel were true?

Lord God, how well I know that I need a Savior and that the Gospel is true! I am sorry for the times I have tried to side step apologizing for my mistakes and confessing my sin to others. By Your Holy Spirit's power, remake my will and give me a humble heart.

Try This: Next time you make a mistake, apologize.

These should learn first of all to put their religion into practice by caring for their own family. 1 Timothy 5:4

Unfinished Business

Susan Bauer describes a congregation's family-like qualities: "They helped when your children were born, and in illness or hardship. They brought casseroles and advice. You laughed and cried together. Together you cooked, cleaned, made banners and music. *They were your family.*"

Church workers and their families are frequently separated from the families in which they grew up. For many, this is a grief. For some, a relief.

Research indicates that some choose church work because of serious unresolved problems in their families-of-origin. Unable to resolve those troubles, they trade their troubled first families for a congregational family.

But the congregation's family-like structure is a gathering of *surrogate* parents, siblings, uncles, cousins, and nieces.

If you are neglecting your family in favor of this family of God, you've probably got uncomfortable, important work to do at home.

Let the family of God, made a reality by Christ's atoning sacrifice, strengthen and support you as you *finish your unfinished business.*

Lord, I know that I have at times neglected my first family in favor of my congregational family. I am sorry that I have left problems untended and business unfinished. Give me the courage and wisdom to know how to address these needs.

Try This: If you need to work with a professional counselor, do so.

We worked night and day in order not to be a burden to anyone while we preached the gospel of God to you. 1 Thessalonians 2:9

Barter System

Janet exploded with pain, anger.

"Dave worked crazy hours as youth minister. Kids called at night, at mealtimes. Parents wanted us there all the time. We never missed a night. We were *always there for them!*

"We loved their kids and did *their* parenting. Now they're not renewing Dave's contract. After all we've done for them!"

A familiar story.

Dave and Janet operated on a silent barter system: *We'll exhaust ourselves for you, and you'll take care of us.*

They depended on the church for emotional, spiritual, and financial well-being, but the system didn't look out for them.

Healthy personal boundaries help you make careful choices about your service—and avoid undue dependence on those you serve.

Strength and security lie in being interdependent.

The Lord who offered up His Son for our salvation promises to meet our every need—and He does it through *many* sources.

Lord, I confess that I have entered into the silent barter system and expected others to meet my needs in exchange for ministry. Help me develop healthy boundaries so I can be an effective servant. Thank You for providing everything I need, and more.

Try This: If you say or think, "After all we've done for them!" you've got some boundary work to do.

A gossip betrays a confidence, but a trustworthy man keeps a secret. Proverbs 11:13

Not Your News to Tell

"I heard Betty was sick. Is it cancer? She always smoked!"

"Poor Jan, I heard Bobby's in trouble again. Was he arrested?"

"How's Sue doing since her sister died? I heard it was AIDS. Did your husband visit her?"

Nosy questions. You hear a lot of them. And you probably know the answers. *But it's not your news to tell.*

You often can pick up news of members—some news and details you'd rather not know. Tragic, sad secrets.

It's a difficult spot. You don't want to discuss it—or lie.

People trust you and your husband with secrets, a trust that must never be betrayed. *Even when questioners profess prayerful intentions.*

So give a short answer without confirming or denying detail. Or suggest the questioner call the person they're asking about. Or refuse details so you honestly can say, "I don't know."

God's enemies have become God's friends because of Christ's death. *That's* news you can tell!

Jesus, sacrifice to God, I am sorry that I have, often with good intentions, told people's secrets and betrayed their confidence. Give me the courage to refuse to gossip. Thank You for the privilege of comforting troubled people with Your love.

Try This: Invent and practice courteous ways to refuse answers to nosy questions.

At this the man's face fell. He went away sad,
because he had great wealth. Mark 10:22

Take No for an Answer

"You *have* to teach VBS," Jean insists. "Look, I'm
exhausted too. And I don't get to say no!"

Some people won't receive a no. They press and
stress—until you say a reluctant yes. You make a half-
hearted commitment and hate to think about keeping it.

It's a guilt trap.

Just because someone makes poor choices, overworks, and hardly has time to go to the bathroom doesn't
mean you have to do the same.

And worst of all, it's easy to guilt trap someone *you're*
asking: You cajole, argue, whine, and beg.

Snap! The guilt trap has another unwilling worker.

Break the coercion habit. Honor the person's decision.
Refuse to refuse a no.

It probably broke His heart, but Jesus allowed the rich
young man to say no. Although He was going to give His
life for the man's salvation, Jesus honored his choice.

Take no for an answer. It's the respectful thing to do.

*Lord, thank You for the many opportunities I have to use
my gifts and abilities in Your service. Teach me to say a firm
no when I must—and a joyful yes when I can. Forgive me for
not honoring others' nos.*

Try This: When you're tempted to cajole and beg,
stop.

How lovely is Your dwelling place, O LORD Almighty! Psalm 84:1

The Best Place

It was the best place to raise your kids and the best house you've ever lived in and the best place to do ministry. You enjoyed the community, liked the schools. It was a great fit.

You didn't know when you left that it was going to occupy such an important place in your memory, but that special place has served as a comparison for all the places that followed.

Since you left, there have been good places, important ministries, dear and wonderful people.

But that was the best place.

Enjoy those wonderful memories and keep track of those dear people. Haul out the photo albums and see proof that God generously met your needs—and more.

Because of Christ's life and death and rising, you will be with God in heaven forever. Christ's death assures it. God's gift of faith enables you to claim it.

The *best best* place is yet to come.

Lord God Almighty! Thank You for my place in heaven and for that wonderful earthly place I remember so fondly. Keep my hope focused on heaven, my faith strong, my joy in You complete.

Try This: Haul out the photographs of your best place and reminisce with thanksgiving.